ROYAL COURT

The Royal Court Theatre presents

ADLER & GIBB

ADLER & GIBB was first performed at the Royal Court Jerwood Theatre Downstairs, Sloane Square, on Friday 13th June 2014.

ADLER & GIBB is a co-commission with the Center Theatre Group.

ADLER & GIBB

by Tim Crouch

Cast
Gibb **Amelda Brown**
Sam **Brian Ferguson**
Louise **Denise Gough**
Student **Rachel Redford**
Child Performers **Eryk Ajdinovski & Sonny Neath; Nico Dietz & Miila Dietz; Lily Mace Horan & George Purves**

Director **Tim Crouch** with **Karl James & Andy Smith**
Designer **Lizzie Clachan**
Lighting Designer **Natasha Chivers**
Composers & Sound Designers **Ben & Max Ringham**
Film **Christine Molloy & Joe Lawlor**
Dialect Coach **Michaela Kennen**
Assistant Director **Caroline Byrne**
Casting Director **Julia Horan CDG**
Casting Deputy **Lotte Hines**
Production Manager **Tariq Rifaat**
Stage Manager **Sophia Dalton**
Deputy Stage Manager **Fran O'Donnell**
Assistant Stage Manager **Sarah Coates**
Stage Management Work Placement **Abigail Lawrence**
Costume Supervisor **Lucy Walshaw**
Chaperone **Elaine Henderson**
Set Built & Painted by **Ridiculous Solutions Ltd**
Other Scenic Elements by **Miraculous Engineering Ltd**

US Film Team
Director of Photography **Joe De Salvo**
Grip **Chris Ingvordsen**
Gaffer **Torkil Stavdal**
Location Manager **Xina Sheehan**
Production Assistant **Tim Duerden**

The filming for this production was supported using public funding by the National Lottery through Arts Council England.

Thanks to Camberwell College of Arts for their collaboration on the website www.adlerandgibb.com: Nisha Gouveia, Stefan Graham, Taylee Morris, Vanessa Periam, Mai Trinh, Tracey Waller & Jane Collins.

The Royal Court and Stage Management wish to thank the following for their help with this production: Paul Rowley, Mary O'Gara, Kirsten Platt, Nature Boy, The Delaware County Historical Association, all the dogs & all their owners, Hotcam for TV Camera & Lighting Equipment.

THE COMPANY

TIM CROUCH (Writer & Director)

FOR THE ROYAL COURT: The Author (& tour); John, Antonio & Nancy (Rough Cut).

OTHER THEATRE INCLUDES: HOST/An Act of Union (Nightingale/Brighton Fringe); what happens to the hope at the end of the evening (Almeida Festival); King Lear (RSC/First Encounter); I, Cinna (The Poet) (RSC/World Shakespeare Festival); The Taming Of The Shrew (RSC/First Encounter); Cadavre Exquis (Kassys/Nature Theatre of Oklahoma/Nicole Beutler/tour); I, Malvolio (Brighton Festival/tour); May (Probe Projects); ENGLAND (Traverse/Whitechapel Gallery/tour); An Oak Tree (Traverse/Soho/tour); Fairymonsterghost (I, Banquo; I, Peaseblossom; I, Caliban) (Unicorn/tour); Kaspar the Wild (Theatre Royal Plymouth/Theatre Royal York/Polka); Shopping For Shoes (NT Education Department tour); My Arm (Traverse/tour).

AWARDS INCLUDE: Prix Italia for Best Adaptation in Radio Drama (My Arm); OBIE Award for Special Citations (An Oak Tree); John Whiting Award (The Author); Scotsman Fringe First, Total Theatre & Herald Archangel Awards (ENGLAND).

AMELDA BROWN (Gibb)

FOR THE ROYAL COURT: My Heart's a Suitcase, Apart from George (& National/tour), Fen/Mouthful of Birds (& Joint Stock).

OTHER THEATRE INCLUDES: Séance on a Sunday Afternoon (Nottingham Lakeside); Hamlet (Haymarket, Basingstoke); Gone to Earth, The Clearing (Shared Experience); A Special Relationship (Theatre Royal York); Abigail's Party (West End); No Way Out (Cochrane); Meat (Theatre Royal, Plymouth); The Cherry Orchard (ETT); Great Balls of Fire (Cambridge); Intimate Death (Gate); Twins, Kafka's Dick, The Relapse, Village Wooing & The Lover, A Midsummer Night's Dream, The Real Thing (Birmingham Rep); Like a Dancer (New End); The Importance of Being Earnest (Mercury, Colchester); A Chaste Maid in Cheapside (Globe); Wishbones, Waiting at the Water's Edge (Bush); Light Shining in Buckinghamshire (National); Beautiful Thing (Donmar/West End); The Swan (Traverse); When We Are Married (West Yorkshire Playhouse); Just Between Ourselves (Bristol Old Vic); Miss Julie (Oldham Coliseum); Our Country's Good, Top Girls (Curve, Leicester); Fire in the Lake, Power of the Dog (Joint Stock tour); Trafford Tanzi, Cider with Rosie (Octagon); Falkland Sound (Belgrade, Coventry); Girl Talk (Soho).

TELEVISION INCLUDES: Casualty, Call the Midwife, Doctors, Waking the Dead, The Bill, Spooks, New Tricks, The Fixer, Ashes to Ashes, Doctors, Miss Marple, Bleak House, Hex II, Derailed, Hidden City, The Quest, Holby City, The 10th Kingdom, Playing the Field, Trial by Jury, The Thin Blue Line, Pie in the Sky, Grange Hill, Back Up, Ellington, Class Act, Soldier Soldier, Sibling Rivalry, Mayhew's London, Minder, Chandler & Co, A Touch of Frost, Love Joy, Peak Practice, Medics, Seconds Out, Shrinks, Capital City, The Rainbow, The Practice, Sherlock Holmes.

FILM INCLUDES: The Boat That Rocked, Harry Potter & the Half-Blood Prince, Outlaw, V for Vendetta, Blood, Candle in the Dark, My Sister in this House, Dakota Road, Spirit, Hope & Glory, Little Dorrit, An English Christmas, Biddy.

RADIO INCLUDES: Sold on eBay, A Harlot's Progress, The Goldilocks Zone, Tess of the D'Urbervilles, Digging, Parklife.

CAROLINE BYRNE (Assistant Director)

THEATRE INCLUDES: By Mr Farquhar (Waterside, Derry); Text Messages: Macbeth (Project Arts Centre); The Recovery Position (Lion & Unicorn); Twizzler Soaked Ecstasy (Bernhard Theatre Studio); The Children (Embassy); Lab Run, Attempts on Her Life (Durham Theatre, Berkeley).

AS ASSOCIATE DIRECTOR, THEATRE INCLUDES: Grounded (Gate).

AS ASSISTANT DIRECTOR, THEATRE INCLUDES: Wendy & Peter Pan (RSC); King Lear (YPS/RSC); Purple Heart (Gate).

AS CO-DIRECTOR, THEATRE INCLUDES: Shakespeare in a Suitcase (RSC).

Caroline is Associate Director at the Gate Theatre and Education Associate Practitioner at RSC.

NATASHA CHIVERS (Lighting Designer)

FOR THE ROYAL COURT: The Mistress Contract, Gastronauts, The Djinns of Eidgah, That Face (& West End).

OTHER THEATRE INCLUDES: 1984 (Headlong/Almeida/West End); War Correspondents (Song/UK tour); Macbeth (National Theatre of Scotland/Broadway); The Green Snake (National Theatre of China);

Praxis Makes Perfect (Neon Neon/National Theatre of Wales); The Radicalisation Of Bradley Manning (National Theatre of Wales); 27, The Wheel, Home: Glasgow, Mary Stuart, The House of Bernard Alba, Empty/The Miracle Man (National Theatre of Scotland); One Monkey Don't Stop No Show, The Village Bike, Happy Days (Crucible, Sheffield); And The Horse You Rode in On (Told By An Idiot); Statement of Regret (National); Sunday in the Park with George (West End); The Wolves in the Walls (National Theatre of Scotland/Improbable); Othello, Dirty Wonderland, Pool (No Water), Tiny Dynamite, Peepshow, Hymns, Sell-Out (Frantic Assembly).

DANCE INCLUDES: Motor Show (LIFT/Brighton Festival); Electric Hotel (Sadler's Wells/Fuel); Electric Counterpoint (Royal Opera House); God's Garden (Arthur Pita/ROH Linbury/tour); Scattered, Broken (Motionhouse/tour/Queen Elizabeth Hall); Run!, Renaissance (Greenwich & Docklands International Festival); Beyond Belief (Legs on the Wall/Carriageworks, Sydney); Encore (Sadler's Wells); The Ballet Boyz (Royal Festival Hall).

OPERA INCLUDES: Zaide (Classical Opera/Sadler's Wells/tour).

AWARDS INCLUDE: Theatre Critics of Wales Award 2014 for Best Lighting Design (Praxis Makes Perfect); UK Theatre Award for Best Design (Happy Days - with Lizzie Clachan); Olivier Award for Best Lighting Design (Sunday in the Park with George).

LIZZIE CLACHAN (Designer)

FOR THE ROYAL COURT: Gastronauts, Jumpy, Wastwater, Our Private Life, Aunt Dan & Lemon, The Girlfriend Experience (& Drum Theatre, Plymouth), On Insomnia & Midnight (& Festival Internacional Cervantino, Guanajuato/Centro Cultural Helénico, Mexico City), Shoot/Get Treasure/Repeat (& National/Out of Joint/Paines Plough), Woman & Scarecrow (& RSC), Ladybird.

OTHER THEATRE INCLUDES: All My Sons (Regent's Park Open Air); A Sorrow Beyond Dreams (Burgtheater, Vienna); Edward II, Port, A Woman Killed with Kindness (National); A Season in the Congo, The Soldier's Fortune (Young Vic); Longing, The Trial of Ubu, Tiger Country (Hampstead); Rings of Saturn (Shauspiel, Cologne); Crave/Illusions (ATC); Happy Days (Crucible, Sheffield); Far Away (Bristol Old Vic); Treasure Island (West End); The Architects, Money, Tropicana, Amato Saltone, Ether Frolics, Dance Bear Dance, The Ballad of Bobby François, The Tennis Show (Shunt); Contains Violence, Absolute Beginners (Lyric, Hammersmith); Julie, Gobbo (National Theatre of Scotland); Factory Girls (Arcola); I'll Be the Devil, Days of Significance, The American Pilot (RSC).

OPERA INCLUDES: Le Vin Herbe (Staatstoper, Berlin); Bliss (Staatsoper, Hamburg).

AWARDS INCLUDE: UK Theatre Award for Best Design (Happy Days - with Natasha Chivers).

Lizzie co-founded Shunt in 1998 and is an Artistic Director of the company.

BRIAN FERGUSON (Sam)

FOR THE ROYAL COURT: The Big Idea: Unusual Unions, Brief Encounters (Rehearsed Reading).

OTHER THEATRE INCLUDES: Money: The Game Show (Bush/Unlimited); The Aztec Trilogy, Richard III, Dunsinane (RSC); Snuff (Arches); Earthquakes in London (National); The Dark Things, Fall (Traverse); The Drawer Boy (Tron); Black Watch, Rupture (National Theatre of Scotland); Observe the Sons of Ulster Marching Towards the Somme (Citizens); Falling (NTS Workshop/Poorboy).

TELEVISION INCLUDES: Our World War, Field of Blood, Doctors, The Prayer, River City, Taggart.

FILM INCLUDES: Residue, Imagine That, The Woods, Voices.

DENISE GOUGH (Louise)

FOR THE ROYAL COURT: O Go My Man (& Out of Joint).

OTHER THEATRE INCLUDES: Desire Under the Elms (Lyric, Hammersmith); Our New Girl (Bush); Ahaverus (RSC); The Painter (Arcola); The Plough & the Stars (Abbey); Jesus Hopped the A Train (Trafalgar Studios); The Birds (Gate, Dublin); Six Characters in Search of an Author (West End/Chichester Minerva); The Grouch (West Yorkshire Playhouse); Someone Else's Shoes (Soho); Everything is Illuminated (Hampstead); Flanders Mare (Sounds); As You Like It, By the Bog of Cats... (West End); The Kindness of Strangers (Liverpool Everyman); Robbers (Tristan Bates).

TELEVISION INCLUDES: Stella, Musketeers, What Remains, Titanic: Blood & Steel, Waking the Dead, Silent Witness, Tom Hurndall, Messiah V, The Commander, Inspector Lynley Mysteries, Tell Me Lies.

FILM INCLUDES: Jimmy's Hall, Hollows, Complicit, The Kid, Robin Hood, Desire, Lecture 21.

AWARDS INCLUDE: Critics' Circle Jack Tinker Award for Most Promising Newcomer.

KARL JAMES (Co-Director)

FOR THE ROYAL COURT: The Author (& tour).

OTHER THEATRE INCLUDES: what happens to the hope at the end of the evening (Almeida Festival); I, Malvolio (Brighton Festival/tour); ENGLAND (Traverse/Whitechapel Gallery/tour); An Oak Tree (Traverse/Soho/tour); My Arm (Traverse/tour); Hamlet, Grace, Mirad, A Boy from Bosnia Pt 1 (Oxford Stage Company); Hamlet (Tokyo Globe); The Idiot (Place).

TELEVISION INCLUDES: Ever Decreasing Circles.

RADIO INCLUDES: Short Cuts, A Different Kind of Justice.

PODCASTS INCLUDE: 2+2=5: Intimate Conversations (premiered at Latitude Festival, 2005-2010).

As director of The Dialogue Project, founded by Karl in response to the events of Sept 11th 2001, he spends most of his time bringing together people with different points of view to help them co-create ideas and solutions. As an advisor, practitioner, negotiator and facilitator of dialogue, evidence of Karl's work can be found in a wide range of learning and work places, from the board rooms and factory floors of global organisations to the staffrooms and classrooms of primary and secondary schools across the UK.

Karl's first book, Say It and Solve It, is published by Pearson this summer.

CHRISTINE MOLLOY & JOE LAWLOR (Film)

THEATRE INCLUDES: Anatomy of Two Exiles, HOPE (Institute of Contemporary Arts, Barclays New Stages); Dedicated (Showroom Gallery); Indulgence (Project Arts Centre); Stalking Realness (Arnolfini); Play-boy, Bull (Arizona State University); Time-Bomb (Dublin Youth); Tom & Vera (Dublin Theatre Festival).

FILM INCLUDES: Who Killed Brown Owl, Moore Street, Revolution, Twilight, Town Hall, Leisure Centre, Now We Are Grown Up, Daydream, Joy, Helen, Tiong Bahru, Mister John.

DVD INCLUDES: Civic Life, Helen, Mister John.

ONLINE WORK INCLUDES: lostcause 1-10 (Expo 2000 Hannover); map50 (Institute of Contemporary Arts); Minute by Minute (Newham Council); Domestic (Shooting Live Artists).

Christine Molloy and Joe Lawlor produce work under the name Desperate Optimists.

RACHEL REDFORD (Student)

THEATRE INCLUDES: Parallel Lines (Chapter Arts Centre/Dirty Protest); A Family Affair (Sherman); Romeo & Juliet (Black Rat Productions); Not the Worst Place (Paines Plough).

FILM INCLUDES: The Riot Club, Nights.

BEN & MAX RINGHAM (Composers & Sound Designers)

FOR THE ROYAL COURT: NSFW, Remembrance Day, The Pride (& West End), The Author.

OTHER THEATRE INCLUDES: Ring (BAC); I Can't Sing!, Blithe Spirit, The Ladykillers, The Full Monty, A Midsummer Night's Dream, Jeeves & Wooster, The Hot House, Les Parents Terribles, What the Butler Saw, Branded, All About My Mother, Democracy, The Rise & Fall of Little Voice, A Christmas Carol, The Little Dog Laughed, Three Days of Rain (West End); Lungs (Schaubuhne); Tartuffe (Birmingham Rep); The Ladykillers (West End/UK tour); A Mad World My Masters, American Trade, Little Eagles (RSC); Paper Dolls, A Taste of Honey, The History Boys, An Enemy of the People, Racing Demon, Hamlet (Crucible, Sheffield); The School for Scandal (Theatre Royal, Bath); Ben Hur (Watermill); Piaf (West End/Buenos Aires); The Duchess of Malfi (Old Vic); The World of Extreme Happiness, Scenes from an Execution, She Stoops to Conquer, Really Old, Like Forty Five, Henry IV pts I & II (National); Painkiller (Lyric, Belfast); My City (Almeida); The Caretaker (Tricycle/tour); The Electric Hotel (Fuel); Glorious (Rajni Shah Productions); Polar Bears, Phaedra (Donmar); Salome (Headlong); Contains Violence (Lyric, Hammersmith); The Lover/The Collection (Comedy); The Architects, Amato Saltone, What If...?, Tropicana, Dance Bear Dance, The Ballad of Bobby Francois, The Pigeon (Shunt).

TELEVISION INCLUDES: Panto.

AWARDS INCLUDE: Off West End Award for Best Sound Design (Ring).

Ben & Max were part of the creative team who accepted an Olivier Award for Best Overall Achievement in an Affiliate Theatre (The Pride). They are associate artists with the Shunt collective & two-thirds of the band Superthriller.

ANDY SMITH (Co-Director)

Andy Smith is a writer and theatre maker who over the last ten years has been making theatre under the name a smith, writing and performing characteristically simple solo works. These include the next two days of everything (2009), all that is solid melts into air (2011) and commonwealth (2012), which was also performed by Tim Crouch at the Royal Court in July 2013 as part of the Open Court season.

Andy has been working with Tim since 2004, co-directing (with Karl James) his plays An Oak Tree (2005), ENGLAND (2007) and The Author (2009). In 2013, Tim and Andy co-wrote and performed what happens to the hope at the end of the evening at the Almeida Theatre.

Andy is currently completing an AHRC-funded practice-as-research PhD at Lancaster University, where he has also taught courses in Contemporary Theatre Practice, Performance Composition and Contemporary European Theatre.

New Season

JERWOOD THEATRE DOWNSTAIRS

17 Jul – 9 Aug
Co-produced with Headlong

the nether

By Jennifer Haley
An intricate crime drama and haunting
sci-fi thriller.

JERWOOD THEATRE UPSTAIRS

Until 28 June
Co-produced with Birmingham Repertory Theatre

khandan (family)

By Gurpreet Kaur Bhatti
A warm and funny play about tradition
and ambition.

1 – 12 July

the art of dying

Written and performed by Nick Payne
A funny and heart-breaking new play about
death, dying and the deceased. A mix of fact
and fiction.

15 – 17 July
The Royal Shakespeare Company presents

four new plays as part of
midsummer mischief

**By Alice Birch, E.V. Crowe, Timberlake
Wertenbaker, Abi Zakarian**
The writers respond to the quote by
Laurel Thatcher Ulrich 'Well-behaved
women seldom make history'.
Sold-out. Returns only.

25 – 26 July
Chris Goode and company in
association with Royal Court Theatre

men in the cities

By Chris Goode
An incendiary piece of experimental
storytelling for two performances ahead of a
run at the Edinburgh Fringe Festival.

Headlong

Innovation Partner

Supported using public funding by
**ARTS COUNCIL
ENGLAND**

THE ENGLISH STAGE COMPANY
AT THE ROYAL COURT THEATRE

The Royal Court is the writers' theatre. It is a leading force in world theatre, finding writers and producing new plays that are original and contemporary. The Royal Court strives to be at the centre of civic, political, domestic and international life, giving writers a home to tackle big ideas and world events and tell great stories.

photo: Stephen Cummiskey

The Royal Court commissions and develops an extraordinary quantity of new work, reading over 3000 scripts a year and annually producing around 14 world or UK premieres in its two auditoria at Sloane Square in London. Over 200,000 people visit the Royal Court each year and many thousands more see our work elsewhere through transfers to the West End and New York, national and international tours, residencies across London and site-specific work, including recent Theatre Local Seasons in Peckham, King's Cross and Haggerston.

The Royal Court's extensive development activity encompasses a diverse range of writers and artists and includes an ongoing programme of writers' attachments, readings, workshops and playwriting groups. Twenty years of pioneering work around the world means the Royal Court has relationships with writers on every continent.

The Royal Court opens its doors to radical thinking and provocative discussion, and to the unheard voices and free thinkers that, through their writing, change our way of seeing.

"With its groundbreaking premieres and crusading artistic directors, the Royal Court has long enjoyed a reputation as one of our most daring, seat-of-its-pants theatres." The Times

"The most important theatre in Europe." New York Times

Within the past sixty years, John Osborne, Arnold Wesker and Howard Brenton have all started their careers at the Court. Many others, including Caryl Churchill, Mark Ravenhill and Sarah Kane have followed. More recently, the theatre has found and fostered new writers such as Polly Stenham, Mike Bartlett, Bola Agbaje, Nick Payne and Rachel De-lahay and produced many iconic plays from Laura Wade's *Posh* to Bruce Norris' *Clybourne Park* and Jez Butterworth's *Jerusalem*. Royal Court plays from every decade are now performed on stage and taught in classrooms across the globe.

Supported by
**ARTS COUNCIL
ENGLAND**

ROYAL COURT SUPPORTERS

The Royal Court has significant and longstanding relationships with many organisations and individuals who provide vital support. It is this support that makes possible its unique playwriting and audience development programmes.

Coutts supports Innovation at the Royal Court. The Genesis Foundation supports the Royal Court's work with International Playwrights. Theatre Local is sponsored by Bloomberg. AlixPartners support The Big Idea at the Royal Court. The Jerwood Charitable Foundation supports emerging writers through the Jerwood New Playwrights series. The Pinter Commission is given annually by his widow, Lady Antonia Fraser, to support a new commission at the Royal Court.

PUBLIC FUNDING
Arts Council England, London
British Council

CHARITABLE DONATIONS
Martin Bowley Charitable Trust
Cowley Charitable Trust
The Dorset Foundation
The Eranda Foundation
Esmée Fairbairn Foundation
Genesis Foundation
The Golden Bottle Trust
The Haberdashers' Company
The Idlewild Trust
Jerwood Charitable Foundation
Marina Kleinwort Trust
The Andrew Lloyd Webber Foundation
John Lyon's Charity
Clare McIntyre's Bursary
The Andrew W. Mellon Foundation
The David & Elaine Potter Foundation
Rose Foundation
Royal Victoria Hall Foundation
The Sackler Trust
The Sobell Foundation
John Thaw Foundation
The Vandervell Foundation
Sir Siegmund Warburg's Voluntary Settlement
The Garfield Weston Foundation
The Wolfson Foundation

CORPORATE SUPPORTERS & SPONSORS
AKA
Alix Partners
American Airlines
Aqua Financial Solutions Ltd
BBC
Bloomberg

Café Colbert
Coutts
Fever-Tree
Gedye & Sons
Kudos Film & Television
MAC
Moët & Chandon
Quintessentially Vodka
Smythson of Bond Street
White Light Ltd

BUSINESS ASSOCIATES, MEMBERS & BENEFACTORS
Annoushka
Auerbach & Steele Opticians
Bank of America Merrill Lynch
Byfield Consultancy
Capital MSL
Cream
Lazard
Vanity Fair
Waterman Group

DEVELOPMENT ADVOCATES
Elizabeth Bandeen
Anthony Burton CBE
Piers Butler
Sindy Caplan
Sarah Chappatte
Cas Donald (Vice Chair)
Celeste Fenichel
Piers Gibson
Emma Marsh (Chair)
Deborah Shaw Marquardt (Vice Chair)
Tom Siebens
Sian Westerman
Daniel Winterfeldt

Supported by
ARTS COUNCIL ENGLAND

Innovation Partner

INDIVIDUAL MEMBERS

MAJOR DONORS
Anonymous
Eric Abraham
Ray Barrell & Ursula Van Almsick
Rob & Siri Cope
Cas Donald
Lydia & Manfred Gorvy
Richard & Marcia Grand
Jack & Linda Keenan
Adam Kenwright
Mandeep Manku
Miles Morland
Mr & Mrs Sandy Orr
NoraLee & Jon Sedmak
Deborah Shaw & Stephen Marquardt
Jan & Michael Topham
Monica B Voldstad

MOVER-SHAKERS
Anonymous
Christine Collins
Jordan Cook
Mr & Mrs Roderick Jack
Duncan Matthews QC
Mr & Mrs Timothy D Proctor
Ian & Carol Sellars

BOUNDARY-BREAKERS
Anonymous
Katie Bradford
Piers & Melanie Gibson
David Harding
Madeleine Hodgkin
Nicola Kerr
Philip & Joan Kingsley
Emma Marsh
Clive & Sally Sherling
Edgar & Judith Wallner
Mr & Mrs Nick Wheeler

GROUND-BREAKERS
Anonymous
Allen Appen & Jane Wiest
Moira Andreae
Mr & Mrs Simon Andrews
Nick Archdale
Charlotte Asprey
Elizabeth & Adam Bandeen
Michael Bennett
Sam & Rosie Berwick
Dr Kate Best
Christopher Bevan
Sarah & David Blomfield
Deborah Brett
Mr & Mrs William Broeksmit
Peter & Romey Brown
Joanna Buckenham
Clive & Helena Butler

Piers Butler
Sindy & Jonathan Caplan
Gavin & Lesley Casey
Sarah & Philippe Chappatte
Tim & Caroline Clark
Carole & Neville Conrad
Andrea & Anthony Coombs
Clyde Cooper
Ian & Caroline Cormack
Mr & Mrs Cross
Andrew & Amanda Cryer
Alison Davies
Roger & Alison De Haan
Matthew Dean
Sarah Denning
Polly Devlin OBE
Rob & Cherry Dickins
Robyn Durie
Glenn & Phyllida Earle
Graham & Susanna Edwards
The Edwin Fox Foundation
Mark & Sarah Evans
Celeste & Peter Fenichel
Margy Fenwick
Beverley Gee
Nick & Julie Gould
Lord & Lady Grabiner
Jill Hackel & Andrzej Zarzycki
Carol Hall
Stephen & Jennifer Harper
Maureen Harrison
Mr & Mrs Sam Haubold
Gordon & Brette Holmes
Kate Hudspeth
Damien Hyland
Suzie & David Hyman
Amanda & Chris Jennings
Melanie J Johnson
Nicholas Jones
Dr Evi Kaplanis
Susanne Kapoor
David P Kaskel & Christopher A Teano
Vincent & Amanda Keaveny
Peter & Maria Kellner
Dominic Kendrick
Steve Kingshott
Mr & Mrs Pawel Kisielewski
Mr & Mrs David & Sarah Kowitz
Daisy & Richard Littler
Kathryn Ludlow
Suzanne Mackie
Dr Ekaterina Malievskaia & George Goldsmith
Christopher Marek Rencki
Mr & Mrs Marsden

Mrs Janet Martin
Andrew McIver
Barbara Minto
Takehito Mitsui
Angelie Moledina
Riley Morris
Peter & Maggie Murray-Smith
Ann & Gavin Neath CBE
Clive & Annie Norton
Jonathan Och & Rita Halbright
Georgia Oetker
James Orme-Smith
Sir William & Lady Vanessa Patey
Andrea & Hilary Ponti
Annie & Preben Prebensen
Paul & Gill Robinson
Andrew & Ariana Rodger
Daniel Romualdez
Corinne Rooney
Sir & Lady Ruddock
William & Hilary Russell
Sally & Anthony Salz
Bhags Sharma
The Michael & Melanie Sherwood Charitable Foundation
Tom Siebens & Mimi Parsons
Andy Simpkin
Anthony Simpson & Susan Boster
Andrea Sinclair & Serge Kremer
Paul & Rita Skinner
Brian Smith
Saadi & Zeina Soudavar
Sue St Johns
The Ulrich Family
Amanda Vail
Constanze Von Unruh
Ian & Victoria Watson & The Watson Foundation
Jens Smith Wergeland
Matthew & Sian Westerman
Mrs Alexandra Whiley
Anne-Marie Williams
Sir Robert & Lady Wilson
Mr Daniel Winterfeldt & Mr Jonathan Leonhart
Katherine & Michael Yates

With thanks to our Friends, Stage-Taker and Ice-Breaker members whose support we greatly appreciate.

Become a Member

The Royal Court has been on the cutting edge of new drama for more than 50 years. Thanks to our members, we are able to undertake the vital support of writers and the development of their plays – work which is the lifeblood of the theatre.

In acknowledgement of their support, members are invited to venture beyond the stage door to share in the energy and creativity of Royal Court productions.

Please join us as a member to celebrate our shared ambition whilst helping to ensure our ongoing success. We can't do it without you.

To join as a Royal Court member from £250 a year, please contact Anna Sampson, Development Manager:
Email: annasampson@royalcourttheatre.com
Tel: 020 7565 5049

www.royalcourttheatre.com

The English Stage Company at the Royal Court Theatre is a registered charity (No. 231242).

Tim Crouch

ADLER & GIBB

and

what happens to the hope
at the end of the evening

by Tim Crouch and Andy Smith

OBERON BOOKS
LONDON

WWW.OBERONBOOKS.COM

First published in 2014 by Oberon Books Ltd
521 Caledonian Road, London N7 9RH
Tel: +44 (0) 20 7607 3637 / Fax: +44 (0) 20 7607 3629
e-mail: info@oberonbooks.com
www.oberonbooks.com

A catalogue record for this book is available from the British
Library.

PB ISBN: 978-1-78319-092-8
E ISBN: 978-1-78319-591-6

Cover: Paul Koudounaris from his book *Heavenly Bodies: Cult
Treasures and Spectacular Saints from the Catacombs*
(Thames and Hudson Ltd MED)

Printed, bound and converted
by CPI Group (UK) Ltd, Croydon, CR0 4YY.

Visit www.oberonbooks.com to read more about all our books
and to buy them. You will also find features, author interviews and
news of any author events, and you can sign up for e-newsletters
so that you're always first to hear about our new releases.

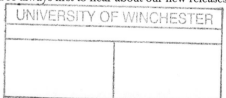

For Ed Vassallo and Ann Wolf

Contents

Adler & Gibb is a co-commission by The Royal Court Theatre, London and Center Theatre Group, Los Angeles.

Adler & Gibb was developed, in part, at the 2013 Sundance Institute Theatre Lab at MASS MoCA.

Thanks

Louise Calf, Sam Troughton, Amanda Monfrooe, Hannah Cabell, Charlie Hoffheimer, Didi O'Connell, Charlie and Clara McWeeny, Amy Ehrenberg, Kaitlin LaValley, Joe Crouch, Alice Brown, Jahnee Lawrence, Educare Small School, Kingston, Janice Paran, Philip Himberg, Christopher Hibma and the Sundance Institute, Kelley Kirkpatrick and the Center Theatre Group, Purni Morell, Laura Collier and the National Theatre Studio, Paul Koudounaris, Jo Hawes, Xina Sheehan and Tim Duerden and Reggie, Mario the dog, Carmela Marner and Matt Munisteri, Pamela Peter and Walter Putryck, Julian Richards, Robin Morley, Julia, Nel, Owen and Joe.

ACT ONE

The stage is almost empty.

As the audience enter, two children (approx 8 years old) are somewhere on the stage. They are doing colouring books or just hanging out. Throughout the play, they will be directed in their actions by a live voice which they hear through headphones that they wear at all times – a kind and attentive voice – the voice of someone rehearsed in the role. When the language in the play becomes too adult, they can listen to music through the headphones.

There is a freedom to the quality of this empty stage. An unformed sense, an open sense in which anything is allowed. A playful sense.

With the audience in, the children sit on chairs at the back of the stage.

A young female STUDENT enters and stands centre stage. She is dressed individually – 'freely' – a canvas satchel with badges and slogans on, for example, a women's movement symbol on her jacket, for example.

The STUDENT takes her place at a lectern.

The STUDENT is a younger version of the character LOUISE.

The STUDENT reads from a formal-looking paper.

The STUDENT speaks into a microphone throughout.

STUDENT   Thank you. Um.

                    Candidate name: Louise Elizabeth Mane – as in lion.

Candidate number: 07523 New Jersey,
Eastern Region.
Date: May 19th twenty oh four. Is that how
you say it? Twenty oh four? Twenty-four?
Two thousand and four?

Um, the declared principles of grading
for this paper are taken from the exam
board's Eastern Region directive found in
their October 1997 guidelines. The scoring
rubric referenced includes the score scale
descriptor from Appendix 2c – "an accurate
and thorough explanation of how an artist or
artifact represents the culture in which it was
produced".

First slide, please.

SAM and LOUISE enter, in robes, facing out.

*The children approach SAM and LOUISE. SAM and LOUISE remove
their robes and hand them to the children. The children sit back down.*

SAM and LOUISE are in underwear.

This presentation is about the late American
artist Janet Adler.

In 1996 Janet Adler was described by the art
critic Dave Hickey as the most 'ferociously
talented and uncompromising voice of her
generation'. She died last year – in May
twenty oh three – the exact date is unknown
– and there have been questions around her
death which I will also try to address in this
paper. I have chosen Adler for my study
because I am an admirer both of her work
and what she represents to me and for my

generation. Janet Adler challenged artistic orthodoxy and has inspired me to be true to myself and to recognize my own creativity as a young woman, and the creative potential and freedom that is within us all.

Next slide.

Lines delivered out, facing out – no adopted accents, no gestures. No actions.

SAM	You're wearing a blue blouse.
LOUISE	I'm wearing a blue blouse.
SAM	You're wearing a blue blouse.
LOUISE	I'm wearing a blue blouse.
SAM	You're wearing a blue blouse.
LOUISE	I'm wearing a blue blouse.
SAM	You're wearing a blue blouse.
LOUISE	I'm wearing a blue blouse.
SAM	You're wearing a blue blouse.

Etc.

LOUISE	I'm wearing a blue blouse.
SAM	Keep that focus.

You're sweating.

LOUISE   It's hot.

SAM   No commentary.

           You're sweating.

LOUISE   I'm sweating.

SAM   You're sweating.

LOUISE   I'm sweating.

SAM   You're sweating

LOUISE   I'm sweating.

SAM   You're sweating.

LOUISE   I'm sweating.

           Can we go into something?

SAM   Louise.

LOUISE   Sam, can we? Before we get out?

SAM   Don't try to be / interesting.

LOUISE   Interesting.

SAM   Don't be / interesting.

LOUISE   I'm not being / interesting.

SAM   Shake your shoulders.

LOUISE   Haah.

SAM   Try the seduction. Scene 14. The loft scene.

LOUISE   Here?

SAM   You want to get out, do it outside?

LOUISE   You want the walk? You want actions?

SAM   Just the lines.

LOUISE   You want the accent?

SAM   Sure. I'll read in.

LOUISE   You want tears?

SAM   I want truth.

LOUISE   Truth is tears.

As the STUDENT reads, the children bring in items of clothing for SAM and LOUISE who put them on.

The children sit back down.

5

STUDENT   Um. A true story. My mom – who is an artist too, amateur, oils – my mom once served Miss Adler in a diner on 2nd Avenue in 1995 and we still have the napkin that Adler, um, doodled on. Here it is! This is the real thing.

The STUDENT presents a Ziplock bag with a napkin in it.

I was only a kid, but it's the first time I remember being aware of – Um. It was just after Adler had turned down a commission from Goldman Sachs and she was in all the papers and – My mom asked Miss Adler to sign the napkin and, although she declined, here is a photo of her seated at her table on that day – wearing her distinctive blue, er, blouse – with that napkin!

The STUDENT presents a photograph.

It's interesting to present this object of belief and to consider what cultural and, um, commercial value this artifact might possess – alongside its photographic authentication.

Next slide.

Speech delivered out, facing out – no gestures, no accents, no actions.

Quicker than is natural.

LOUISE   "Oh, honey. Don't you feel it, do you? It will all end with us, you know, with only us. You and me. You know that too, don't you? We will be like climbing partners roped together. If one of us goes, then they will pull the other with them. Gladly down into the crevasse."

SAM	Tears?
LOUISE	I can't.
SAM	Jesus, Louise, she's –
LOUISE	"…Gladly down into the crevasse. Say something."
SAM	"Say something."
LOUISE	"Say something."
SAM	We worked this.
	"Your voice is like heat."
LOUISE	"The blood rushes to those parts of the body and I am light-headed."
SAM	"I should go home."
LOUISE	"You are home."
SAM	"Really?"
LOUISE	"Don't you feel it? Your journey is over."

They kiss. Kiss kiss kiss.

SAM	What's blocking you in this scene? You still scared of the kiss? Is that it? Fake the kiss.

LOUISE	You can't fake a kiss.
SAM	Sure you can. Be clear about your objective. What do you want here? What do you want? Identify your obstacle and use your intention to overcome the obstacle. Do what you want to get what you want.
	You're avoiding me.
LOUISE	I'm avoiding you.
SAM	You're avoiding me.
LOUISE	I'm avoiding you.
SAM	You're avoiding me.
LOUISE	I'm avoiding you.
SAM	You're avoiding me.
LOUISE	I'm avoiding you.
SAM	I'm switching off the engine.
LOUISE	You're switching off the engine.
SAM	No, I'm just saying I'm switching off the –
LOUISE	I knew that.

SAM   Make the most –

LOUISE   I knew that.

SAM   How you feeling?

LOUISE   Nervous.

SAM   Keep that.

As the STUDENT reads, the children take more articles of clothing to SAM and LOUISE who put them on.

LOUISE will wear under garments – as if getting ready to put a costume on over them. She will put on a wig cap – and insert 'fillers' into her bra. SAM will wear regular clothes.

The children sit down again.

STUDENT   Janet Adler died last year – in May, twenty
               three. 2003. The circumstances of her death
               prompted media speculation about the
               nature of her relationship with her partner
               Margaret Gibb. Gibb collaborated with
               Adler on much of her later work. In 1998,
               the critic Arthur Danto described Gibb's
               influence as 'negatory' and has even hinted
               that she was in some way responsible
               for Adler's later 'deformalisation'. Danto
               describes Adler's work as 're-normalising the
               phenomenology of production – away from
               a specialized form and towards a naturalized
               impulse.'

Slide.

In 1999, the two women walked away from the contemporary art world – issuing the slogan: 'Shoot the wounded. Save yourselves.'

Slide, please.

LOUISE and SAM facing out, no gesture, no actions.

SAM   Unreal.

LOUISE   Look at this place. This fog. Look at the trees. Look at the size of those roots.

SAM   Feels good to be here at last. Get out of the vehicle. Dig around. Advance the work.

LOUISE   Find the truth.

SAM   Find the truth.

LOUISE   Who would live here? Who would want this?

SAM   Use that.

LOUISE   Should I put a pencil behind my ear, you think?

SAM   There's nobody here, right?

LOUISE	They did phone.
SAM	But you said they didn't speak to anyone.
LOUISE	They said it's derelict, it's – Don't go on ahead like that. Hey. Slow down.
	I don't have the footwear.
SAM	It's chained.
LOUISE	Don't just walk ahead.
SAM	We could climb it.
LOUISE	You sure this is it?
SAM	I recognize the gate.
LOUISE	How do you know?
SAM	Look and look.
LOUISE	It's an old photo.
SAM	It's rusted.
LOUISE	You sure?
SAM	It's the same one.
LOUISE	I'm not dressed for this.
SAM	So take it off.

LOUISE   I don't climb gates. I'm being bitten to death.
           There's no signal. Have you got a signal?
           Aren't we a little old for this? Do we have a
           hand-held, you know, a fan – a hand-held –
           This heat. This fog. I'll wait in the RV. Tell me
           when you find a way through. I said / I'll –

SAM   The lock is stiff.

LOUISE   Don't go off like that.

SAM   No one's been here.

LOUISE   Sure?

SAM   Give me a hand up.

LOUISE   What?

SAM   A boost.

LOUISE   My costume.

SAM   Hup.

LOUISE   Jumping around like a monkey.

SAM   There's a building.

LOUISE   There is?

SAM   It's overgrown.

LOUISE   Shouldn't you be filming this? Isn't that
                the point? Are there lights on? Is there
                movement? Can't see a damn thing, this air –

SAM   Quiet!

A child gets up and places a tape machine or CD player on the stage and presses play. The sound of the forest. The child sits down.

LOUISE   Shaking like a leaf!

SAM   I thought I saw something.

LOUISE   Someone?

SAM   An animal?

LOUISE   What is there here? Mountain lions? Are we
                going to get eaten alive? Are we crazy? Do
                we have a gun?

SAM   In the flight case.

LOUISE   Seriously?

SAM   Never used one?

LOUISE   I'm from New Jersey.

SAM   No guns in New Jersey?

LOUISE   What are we doing with this?

SAM   Adam said.

LOUISE   What the hell.

SAM   To protect you.

LOUISE   From what?

SAM   Autograph hunters.

LOUISE   Ha!

SAM   Don't point it.

LOUISE   You talking to me?

SAM   Seriously, Lou, don't point it.

LOUISE   Whole place smells of death.

SAM   Go into that fear. The fear is good. It's alive.

LOUISE   Ha. Hah-hah. Haaah.

The child gets up and switches off the sound and takes the player away.

               You want some?

SAM   Sure.

SAM and LOUISE snort deeply.

LOUISE   I'm not climbing. I don't climb.

SAM   That's the house. Or was the / house.

LOUISE   I can feel / her.

SAM   Ruins.

LOUISE   I can sense her, already. She stood here. She
                knew this view. She knew the smell of this
                air. It's like a vibration.

SAM   Use it.

LOUISE   Am I talking differently? You want me to go
                into her? You want me to do the voice?

SAM   I'll get the camera.

LOUISE   Quiet a minute.

                Did you hurt yourself?

SAM   On the fence.

LOUISE   Looks nasty.

SAM   It's nothing.

LOUISE   Looks bad.

SAM   Kiss it better.

LOUISE   Don't push your luck.

                Go on then.

SAM   What?

LOUISE   Get the cutters or whatever. The blow torch,
             the jack hammer, or whatever.

SAM   There's no one around.

LOUISE   My clothes are stuck to me.

SAM   The house ain't going nowhere.

LOUISE   Have to peel them off.

*As the STUDENT reads, the children bring shoes for SAM and LOUISE, who
put them on. The children help with the laces and return to their seats.*

STUDENT   Janet Adler devoted the last years of her life
             to erasing the traces of her artistic output.
             In the year before she left New York she
             bought back a number of her major works
             and supervised their destruction. These
             'dematerialisations', as they became known,
             were celebrated in Karl Hauptmann's
             Academy award-winning documentary *the
             realm of possibility* – a title taken from Adler's
             work of the same name commissioned for
             Greenpeace in 1988.

             Despite never claiming to be an artist, Adler
             was named by *Esquire* magazine in 1999
             as among 'Fifty People Who Have Made a
             Difference'. The French/Bulgarian feminist
             critic Julia Kristeva described Adler as
             popularising the 'abject' – um, a body of
             work situated on the margins of symbolic
             order and between the concepts of both
             object and subject.

At the time of her death, it was estimated that she had made over 9000 pieces, a tiny fraction of which are recorded. A series of hand-written diagrams, *who can say how things were in ages past,* Work #1667, were sold at Sotheby's New York last month for $215,000.

Slide.

The performances are still directed out, no gesture, no action. This sequence faster than is natural.

SAM   Come on.

LOUISE   Quicker.

SAM   Come on.

LOUISE   Quicker.

SAM   There yes, yes there, yes yes.

LOUISE   Quicker.

SAM   Yes there.

LOUISE   Come on.

SAM   I am a fucking monkey.

LOUISE   Oh, please.

SAM   Monkey man.

LOUISE   Jesus.

SAM   Monkey fucker.

LOUISE   Cut it out.

SAM   I'll fuck you, little monkey.

LOUISE   Fuck's sake.

SAM   Yes yes there yes.

LOUISE   Careful.

SAM   Take the banana.

LOUISE   Quiet, Jesus, there could be –

SAM   What?

LOUISE   It could be. Oh.

SAM   You want your banana?

LOUISE   I want you to hurry up.

SAM   Oh fuck, fuck.

LOUISE   Keep your voice down.

SAM   No one can hear us.

LOUISE   Shh.

SAM   No one can hear us.

LOUISE   Careful.

SAM	Yeah.
LOUISE	You're pushing me. Careful.
SAM	Shut up a minute!

The actors speak at normal speed.

Look.

A child has crossed the stage and stands between SAM and LOUISE, facing out.

Don't move.

LOUISE	Oh.
SAM	Oh, man. That is beautiful.
LOUISE	Beautiful.
SAM	It's watching us. Was it watching us you think?
LOUISE	It was watching us. In the mist.
SAM	Does it know what we're doing?
LOUISE	Don't make a move.
SAM	How long has it been there?
LOUISE	Quiet.

It won't hurt us, will it?

SAM   Oh, man. Look at us!

LOUISE   Don't laugh.

SAM   Chk chk.

LOUISE   Shh.

SAM   See if it comes closer.

LOUISE   Leave it.

SAM   Hey hey.

LOUISE   Shut the fuck up.

SAM   It's not scared.

LOUISE   Hello, little one.

SAM   Look at its eyes.

LOUISE   You are so beautiful, aren't you? Aren't you?

A held moment.

The child returns to their seat.

SAM   That was so fucking beautiful.

LOUISE   You scared it.

SAM   I didn't.

LOUISE   You moved.

SAM	I did not.
LOUISE	It's like it saw into me. You know. I could sense it looking into me.

LOUISE and SAM speak slightly faster than normal. Facing out.

SAM	Come on.
LOUISE	Get off me.
SAM	What?
LOUISE	Pull your pants up.
SAM	Really?
LOUISE	What was I thinking?
SAM	This is wilderness.
LOUISE	It could have been anyone.
SAM	The middle of nowhere.
LOUISE	A photographer.
SAM	It's cool.
LOUISE	It's not cool. It's work. It's a working relationship. You show some respect. I am a married woman. How dare you lay your hands on me. How dare you? You think for one minute you can – Don't confuse your purpose. I am the money. You're here for me. This is my idea. You do what I say.

SAM   It's a / great idea.

LOUISE   You want me to tell Adam? You want me to
             tell him? You want my husband to find out
             he's paying for his wife to be fucked by her
             coach? You want that?

SAM   You are the money. I am the monkey.

             Breathe.

LOUISE   Hah ha haaaaaaah.

SAM   You have the responsibility for the energy
             you bring.

LOUISE   Take your hands away.

SAM   You have – there is – you've built a wall
             around you. See how much it takes to
             remove just one brick from that wall. And
             what a change that makes. One brick at a
             time, Lou. One brick, see.

LOUISE   You're the wrong sex, anyway.

SAM   Huh?

LOUISE   I need to fuck a dyke.

SAM   I admire your method!

LOUISE   They were queer.

SAM   No shit.

LOUISE   So?

SAM   So fake it.

LOUISE   I need to feel that.

SAM   Are you saying you never –

LOUISE   What?

SAM   You know.

LOUISE   I'm Adam's girl.

SAM   Yeah, like he never?

LOUISE   Never what?

SAM   With the boys.

LOUISE   What are you saying?

SAM   It's Hollywood.

LOUISE   We're happily married.

SAM   Whatever gets you off.

LOUISE	Do we know any dykes?
SAM	Head of Payroll. 2nd AD. Half of wardrobe.
LOUISE	Seriously?
SAM	Seriously.
LOUISE	You're bleeding. There are wipes in the truck.
SAM	Be right back.
LOUISE	Bring the cameras.
	Bring everything.
	Bring the insect repellant. On the back seat.
	And a beer.
	Where are you?
	Where are you?
	Hey.
	Sam.
	Hey.

As the STUDENT reads, a child sweeps a smoke machine around the stage.

STUDENT	Janet Adler was born in 1943 in Buchenwald concentration camp in Germany. With the liberation of the camp in April 1945, Adler and her mother moved to Vienna before emigrating here to New Jersey in 1958 at the age of fifteen. She never lost a slight German accent and her foreignness is thought to have influenced the syntax of her work.
	Adler studied graphic design at the Pratt Institute, New York. Her early work paid attention to what the art historian Robert Hughes called 'the fault lines in the topography of her childhood'. In 1967 she made an attempt on her life by taking an overdose of barbiturates. She said that at the time she had felt more intimacy with the dead than with the living.
LOUISE	Don't go off. Don't just go off.
SAM	You sent me.
LOUISE	I couldn't see you.
SAM	Here.
LOUISE	What is it?
SAM	A grinder. Stand away from the gate.
LOUISE	We don't know what's in there.
SAM	Nothing's in there. There's nothing.
LOUISE	How do you know?

SAM   Stand back.

LOUISE   Try phoning one last time.

SAM   No signal.

LOUISE   Where did she go?

SAM   Dead.

LOUISE   Wouldn't we have heard?

SAM   She wanted out.

LOUISE   Wouldn't there be a record?

SAM   Couldn't live with herself.

LOUISE   She must be dead, right?

SAM   If she's alive we're in trouble.

LOUISE   Fucking A!

SAM   We go in, we work, we nourish your process,
                we dig around, we film, you know. This is for
                you. We take what we can and we leave. It's
                loud.

LOUISE covers her ears.

LOUISE   I should change out of this.

LOUISE uncovers her ears.

                I said I should change out of this.

SAM   I said it wasn't the sort of place for those
             clothes.

LOUISE   I said I wanted to look right.

SAM   Authentic.

LOUISE   In character.

SAM   Sure.

LOUISE   The hair.

SAM   No one is here.

LOUISE   It's for me, then.

SAM   Yeah, but that's a nice blouse.

LOUISE   Of course it's a nice blouse. Vintage.

SAM   Wear it then.

LOUISE   Nineteen seventy-six. It's identical.

SAM   You look good.

LOUISE   I look fabulous.

             The fog has gone.

             Don't move.

SAM and LOUISE snort deeply.

SAM   We're in.

As the STUDENT reads, the children give SAM more clothes to put on.
A child opens a beer and gives it to LOUISE. She shares it with SAM.

A child brings a piece of scenery onto the stage, for example.

As the play progresses, gradually, the children will 'build' a set – not of
a derelict house in the middle of rural nowhere, but of a room in a New
York loft apartment from the mid-Seventies. Stage management can help
them in this task throughout.

This set will be more like a film set – designed to favour one camera
angle. This film set is not completed until towards the end of the play.

As the STUDENT reads, LOUISE exits the stage.

As the STUDENT reads, GIBB enters – dressed ordinary.

As the STUDENT reads, a child stands next to GIBB.

STUDENT   In 1976 Adler met the young political
           science graduate Margaret Gibb, with whom
           she was to spend the rest of her life. Gibb
           was working for a women's collective in
           Delaware County, New York, but the two
           met at a private showing of outsider art at
           the X Gallery in Greenwich Village, curated
           by Robert Perryman. Adler wrote movingly
           about their first encounter, 'love became
           manifest as a thing undone'.

           Slide.

           Originally from Pennsylvania, Gibb
           experienced an abusive Christian Scientist
           upbringing and left home at the age of 15.
           In an interview with *Village Voice* in 1989 she
           stated that, with no interest in reproduction,

she had funded her way through college
by donating her eggs to early medical
research into fertility treatment at Columbia
University. "They can have 'em all", she is
quoted as saying.

Adler and Gibb became inseparable. They
were a familiar sight in lower Manhattan,
both dressed identically and eccentrically,
often in male clothing. Andy Warhol
immortalized them in 1986 in a triptych of
photographic silk screens entitled *girls, girls,
girls*.

Slide.

After Adler had met Gibb, her art practice
moved away from the abstract expressionism
of her early career – and into a practice of
ideas. Influenced by the Fluxus movement,
they became united in their desire to
integrate art and everyday life.

Um.

Under Adler's guidance, they started to
make work together – most famously, the
series of instructional pieces entitled *ourselves
from a great height*. Three sections of this
series were pieced together from incomplete
transcripts by Scott Berg in his biographical
essay on Adler entitled 'False Endings'. The
dedication to this series was a linguistic
canon made from words suggested to Adler
by the random pattern of ants on the surface
of a sidewalk in Brooklyn Heights in June
1984. The canon, subsequently published by

Berg, was sent to Margaret Gibb in the form of a private love letter.

Slide.

SAM, GIBB and the child, facing out. No gestures, no actions.

GIBB   You think I'm going to tickle you with this, is that it? Think I'm going to give you a little ickle, a tickle, jump right out of my skin, you made me, could have dropped down dead and then where would I be?

SAM   I'm sorry.

GIBB   Oh that's that, then, that's okay, then, that's fixed it, that's fixed it fine, just fine, swell. Just swing on by and do whatever, stand in my house, in my house, why don't you, with what you got in your hand, some cosh is it? Some hickory stick. Going to cosh me, clap me out with your high school gang, your buddies, with your, whatever? And then sorry does it, does it? fixes it? Oops, look, smashed it all up, so sorry, so so sorry, old bird –

SAM   No –

GIBB   – you won't care, will you, old bird, old piece of – That wash, will it, that fix it all? This is private property, private property, this is not for you, get it? get it?

SAM   Look –

GIBB   Well just wander in, waltz in without, without
              any –

SAM   – look, shit, I'm –

GIBB   Yeah, shit, it is shit, isn't it, it really is shit.
              More shit for you, though, by the looks of it,
              all things considered, yes more shit, yes, I'd
              say definitely more shit for you on the scales,
              your, what do you call it, your balance, your
              scale of shit is certainly more, is weighing
              down mine – You certainly have the shitty
              end of the stick, the shit stick, the shitty shit
              stick, the end with all the shit on it. I have
              the end without the shit. No shit on my
              hands. Look, see any shit, no, you don't, by
              golly.

              By shit I don't mean shit. I mean trouble.

              By stick I don't mean stick. I mean gun.

              I mean gun.

SAM   Yes.

GIBB   Do you think I'm crazy?

SAM   Gun.

GIBB   Well I'm not crazy, not one ounce. Sharp as
              a thorn. Super sharp. Sharper.

SAM   Of course. I'm sorry.

GIBB   Think you can just do what the hell, what the
              hell?

SAM   Good boy. Good boy. Could you – Quite a
              beast you have there. He's a big one.

GIBB   Down, Boy. Out.

The child returns to their seat.

SAM   Are you Miss Gibb? Miss Margaret Gibb?
              Only, we thought –

GIBB   What's going on here?

SAM   There was an arrangement.

GIBB   Was there?

SAM   Yes there was.

GIBB   There was, was there.

SAM   Yes.

GIBB   Well that's always nice to know.

SAM   Yes.

GIBB   Always nice for things to be arranged, isn't it,
            like flowers or funerals or – What else, things
            like this? Do things like this get arranged?

SAM   Well, this wasn't.

GIBB   Wasn't what?

SAM   Arranged. Not this. Not exactly this. I mean
            – Would you mind, only –

GIBB   I'm aiming straight at your balls and I would
            dearly love, oh I would so dearly yes, I mind
            a lot, I mind.

SAM   Okay. Just, it's very hard to – to explain with –

            Can I put this down?

GIBB   Where's that accent from?

SAM   Southern California.

            Is that a tree? Is that a real tree?

SAM points at a piece of stage furniture brought on by the children.

A child fetches a twelve-gauge shotgun and places it in GIBB's hand.

The child returns to their seat.

GIBB   Who made the arrangement?

SAM   Through the gallery.

GIBB   The gallery, was it.

SAM   Yes.

GIBB   Who?

SAM   Mr Harper. Adam Harper.

GIBB   Never heard of him.

SAM   But –

GIBB   Show me.

SAM   An email.

GIBB   Oh. An email.

SAM   Yes.

GIBB   I don't do that.

SAM   Your agent?

GIBB   I don't do that.

SAM   No.

GIBB   Harper would've said.

SAM   They said they'd set things up.

GIBB   Who?

SAM   The legal team.

GIBB   What?

SAM   The company.

GIBB   Which company?

SAM   Viacom.

GIBB   Is it a phone company?

SAM   Viacom?

GIBB   I don't have a phone.

SAM   The media company. You know.

GIBB   It doesn't ring any bells, media.

SAM   The film company. About the film.

GIBB   Is that someone moving around upstairs? Is
              it? Who's up there? I come home and find
              I'm being invaded, is that it? Gate busted,
              window smashed. My belongings. How
              many of you are there? I will defend myself.

GIBB raises the gun to shoot – aiming straight out.

              You hurt?

SAM   It's nothing.

GIBB   You're bleeding /all down –

SAM   Just a nick. Caught it /on some –

GIBB   Should clean it up. Don't leave it open. Close
               it up. This air is bad. What you bring me?

SAM   What?

GIBB   In the bag.

SAM   This is equipment.

GIBB   It looks heavy.

SAM   Yes.

GIBB   Is it for me?

SAM   I should have brought something. I have
               cigarettes. From the plane.

GIBB   What plane?

SAM   We flew.

GIBB   Flew where?

SAM   From LA.

GIBB   Fancy that.

SAM   We rented a vehicle. We thought it was
               empty. From the outside it looks empty. We
               thought something must have happened and
               we didn't, that we hadn't been informed.

GIBB   That would be fine.

SAM	What?
GIBB	Whatever you can spare.
SAM	Sure.
GIBB	It's customary for visitors to bring things. They don't have to – I'm perfectly all right on my own. But it's customary, an act of politeness, you understand, and act of humanity, for christ's sake. For christ's sake.

As the STUDENT reads, a child brings on a sledge hammer and hands it to SAM. A child drags on a heavy hold-all and gives it to SAM. A child brings on a small metal flight case and gives it to SAM. A child puts a camera around SAM's neck.

A child applies fake blood to SAM's arm.

The children bring in another piece of scenery.

STUDENT	Writing to her publisher, Martin Helman, in 1981, Janet Adler said that, in Margaret Gibb, she had found her life's audience and that she didn't need any other. She wrote movingly, "The store window is shuttered. The work is now just a life lived."
	Adler & Gibb tattooed each other with identical symbols. I have the same symbol in the same place! Look! Look!

The STUDENT shows her forearm.

	Um.

When asked to contribute to the US Pavilion at the 1984 Venice Biennale, Adler & Gibb presented a film of a pack of sibling dogs ravenously devouring the flesh of their parents. At the end of the Biennale, Adler and Gibb destroyed all known prints of this film. The negative, however, is currently owned by the Swiss banking giant UBS.

Slide, please.

SAM   You don't make it easy. We had to ask at the gas station. The gas station? The woman gave us the wrong directions. Sent us back onto the highway.

GIBB   She did, did she?

SAM   We nearly missed it, the computer doesn't have it, doesn't even have this, this road, this what is it, not road, track. Runs out beyond the village, miles back. There's just a blank. They should fix that. This place is – Get them to come out and map it so people know how to – They will, you know. They don't want there to be gaps. They're doing it to the surface of the moon. Click and drag the little man down and have a look around some crater.

Little green man.

GIBB   That a camera?

SAM   Could I –

GIBB   No.

SAM   Just where you are – Just –

GIBB   You don't. You dare / and I'll –

SAM   I'm not a photographer / just a –

GIBB   You dare –

SAM   – document, a special feature –

GIBB   No record.

SAM   To capture –

GIBB   Nothing. No.

SAM   This stuff is awesome. You have a real
                    Aladdin's cave in here. A wilderness. This
                    looks like it hasn't changed, not changed for,
                    for years. Just the forest, er, the forest coming
                    in. Awesome. We thought you were – We
                    thought this was – You comfy in here? Aren't
                    you scared? Who helps you? How do you
                    survive here in this place?

GIBB   I work in a gas station.

SAM   Oh.

*As SAM speaks, a child replaces the sledgehammer with a plastic fish, for
example. The substitutions can become more outlandish and theatrical.*

GIBB   Are you a thief, a thug?

SAM   Oh, God, no. No. I can't believe you didn't
           know, that no one told you. I'm a – I work
           in the industry – I'm a consultant, a coach,
           an acting, um, coach, kind of adviser – I've
           worked with some really big – We are – there
           is a huge fascination with – with this place,
           with you and your – your partner's - A huge
           interest in the public, a hunger, if you like,
           to know about – what happened to you after
           Janet's – since her passing – to understand
           the – how you, you know, worked and lived
           together and – How long has it been now?
           Ten years since – since Janet passed? Please
           can I put this down? My arm is –

GIBB   Clean it up.

SAM   Yes.

GIBB   What's with the equipment? Is it for your
           acting lessons?

SAM   You won't believe.

GIBB   Getting pretty desperate.

SAM   What?

GIBB   Worse than a thief.

*As she talks, a child replaces GIBB's gun with an inflatable baseball
bat, for example.*

GIBB   When we came here, when we arrived here,
           when we built this place with our hands, with
           our hands, we posted signs in the woods –
           painted them ourselves – saying 'Please go

away' and 'Have you not had enough?' – but
they kept getting stolen, put up for auction,
traded, you name it. So we put up the fence.
Now, I think the gate was locked. What does
a locked gate mean to you? What does it say
to you? To me it says you don't come in, it
says, you mind your own business, it says,
take your huge public interest and – Now,
I don't like the locks, but until they invent
decency and deference and respect for other
people's lives and wishes, then that's what I
think a locked gate means to me. What film?

SAM   They're making a film. About your partner.
             About Janet.

GIBB   No they're not.

*A child replaces the plastic fish, for example, with an inflatable Trident,
for example.*

SAM   You don't know. We thought you were dead,
             you understand.

GIBB   I am dead.

SAM   This is complex.

GIBB   Try me.

SAM   So, three years back, 2011, yeah, three years -
             in Minneapolis, there was a show – a show of
             the work. Organised by Adam Harper – you,
             know, Adam? Your work. Janet's work. You
             didn't know? They didn't tell you?

GIBB   Go on.

SAM   It was her idea, really. Louise. Louise Mane.
               The actress. His wife.

GIBB   He has a wife?

SAM   She's been a fan of yours since high school.

GIBB   How old is she?

SAM   Louise? Young. 28?

GIBB   Harper's my age.

SAM   He's a very powerful man.

               She's an actress.

GIBB   Go on.

SAM   There was, well, it was a success, the show –
               putting it mildly. I think they – Adam – just
               thought of it as a tax write-off – but it was
               mad. Unexpected. Made a ton of money.
               Very minimalist. A lot of the film stuff – a
               collection of the banner art. The written
               material, the instructions. Stuff of hers – of
               yours – they thought had been destroyed
               but Adam had it, he still had it, in a – in
               a – a warehouse. That show toured. Caught
               the imagination. They sold a ton of stuff –
               prints and stuff, postcards, coffee cups – the
               banners. The originals go for thousands,
               tens of thousands. Hundreds. Her work is
               everywhere now. Your work. There was a
               piece in Time magazine. You didn't know?

Went to New York, Chicago, LA, where
they started to talk about the idea of a film.
Adler's life and death – the true story, you
know, her death, the mystery. He, Adam,
he referenced that Schnabel movie – about
Basquiat. My dad worked on that movie. You
seen that? Pretty cool. A lot of big art players
put money into that and they saw their
investment return like 100 fold because the
prices went through the roof, man, through
the roof. The film made it, see. People were
forgetting and then the film and, boom. It's
the same with this. He puts the money up
front. He puts his wife in the movie. He owns
the art and, boom. Everyone wins.

As the STUDENT reads, a child pulls on a table, for example.

A child brings a stage flat on, for example.

A child removes GIBB's 'gun'.

As the STUDENT reads, SAM exits the stage.

As the STUDENT reads, LOUISE enters, transformed into Adler – clothes, wig, make-up.

LOUISE is carrying a shovel in one hand.

A moment between 'Adler' and GIBB.

STUDENT   In 1981 Janet Adler and Margaret Gibb
purchased a celebrated portrait of art critic
Clement Greenberg by the painter Leon
Golub. They then proceeded to publicly
eat the work over the course of two days in
their studio in Park Slope. This installation,

called *The Art Is In Us*, was a reference to
John Latham's eating of Greenberg's book
Art and Culture. It caught the imagination of
the international press and began a long-term
relationship with the celebrated gallerist
Adam Harper. Adler parted company with
Harper in 1997 with an acrimonious law
suit concerning the move by Harper to
trademark their name and the unauthorized
use of kinetic art work #1766 in an
advertising campaign for General Motors.

In 1999 Adler & Gibb issued a manifesto
entitled *there are now enough objects*.

Slide.

With the presentation of the manifesto,
Adler & Gibb withdrew from the public
eye. They moved to a house they had built
on an isolated tract of forested land and set
about self-sufficiency. Paul Goldberger in
the *New York Times* described the house as
sitting like a photographic negative in the
landscape – a perfect example of nominative
architecture, marking it equal to the subject
of its environment.

Slide.

The house became the focus for their life and
their relationship. Tragically, they enjoyed
only three years of their newfound seclusion
before Janet Adler's sudden death last
year, in May 2003, at the age of 59. Much
speculation has been had about the nature of
Adler's death – with some critics suggesting
that her relationship with Gibb could not

withstand and that Gibb was in some way responsible.

Slide, please.

LOUISE and GIBB turn in on each other.

The performances are gradually becoming more dimensional.

GIBB   Oh, darling. Were you just upstairs? Was it you, darling? Was that you clumping around? Is that where you were, all this time? All those years, is it now? I thought you were dead. Why didn't you come down? Were you playing with me? What you got in your hand? You dig yourself out with that? Is that it? You clever girl! I was going to. I promise I was going to. Here, Boy. Come see who's back! Boy sat by you for weeks, he did. Look how old he's gotten. There's only us two left. Oh, honey. Honey. This place has gone bad. A man is bleeding here. When you went. Why didn't I come with you? Oh god, oh god. I'm sorry. Let's get out of this place. Let's start again. Take me back, will you? Take me with you? I've been missing you. You been missing me? Oh, god, honey, I'm not dressed right. I've let myself go. Don't look at me, don't. I'm a mess. A mess! I'm ashamed. You still love me, don't you? Look, Boy, look who's here!

The child has come on and now approaches LOUISE. The child looks at LOUISE. The child looks at GIBB.

What?

GIBB reaches out to LOUISE and then suddenly recoils. The child stays on stage.

Wait.

Did I invite you?

LOUISE   In high school I had your picture on my wall.

GIBB   Well?

LOUISE   I was obsessed with you.

GIBB   Did I?

LOUISE   You and Janet –

GIBB   Let me see.

LOUISE   – gave me such hope –

GIBB   Racking my brain, here.

LOUISE   – the way you lived.

GIBB   I forget.

LOUISE   I adored you.

GIBB   It has slipped my mind.

LOUISE   I have your tattoo.

LOUISE shows her forearm.

GIBB   Are you listening?

LOUISE   Look!

GIBB   Mute, am I?

LOUISE   I freaking studied you!

GIBB   Did I send you an invitation?

LOUISE   I dressed like you.

GIBB   Did I request the pleasure of your company?

LOUISE   I went to pieces when Janet died.

GIBB   Did you RSVP?

LOUISE   I can't believe I am standing here with you.

GIBB   Did you even think?

LOUISE   We thought you were dead!

GIBB   Well?

LOUISE   I was your biggest fan!

GIBB   What happened to you?

LOUISE   I want to give this back to you.

GIBB   Well?

LOUISE	My gift.
GIBB	Gift?
LOUISE	I've come to rescue you, Margaret.
GIBB	Did I send out a distress signal? Did I? I forget. Did I send up a flare? Did I leave a trail of breadcrumbs? Did I international SOS save my soul? Remind me? Did I at any moment – to your recollection – present myself as in any way, any conceivable way, being in need of rescue? Is that your jacket?
LOUISE	Yes.
GIBB	Would you take that jacket off?
LOUISE	There's nothing on the label. *(She calls.)* Sam.
GIBB	Where did you find it?
LOUISE	I'm not going to damage it. *(She calls.)* Sam.
GIBB	It's not yours. It's not yours. Help. Stop thief. Rape. Rape.
	What gift?
LOUISE	Watch.

LOUISE adopts a slight Austrian accent – a perfect impersonation.

> "It will all end with us. You and me. You know that too, don't you? We will be like

climbing partners roped together. If one of us goes, then they will pull the other with them. Gladly down into the crevasse."

GIBB   Who told you that?

LOUISE   It's in / a letter.

GIBB   Was that a letter to you, was it? Was it?

LOUISE   That / letter was –

GIBB   Was that letter a public letter?

LOUISE   You didn't go down the crevasse, / did you?

GIBB   A letter for the / public domain?

LOUISE   She fell on her own, / didn't she?

GIBB   Written for a newspaper, / was it?

LOUISE   You watched / her?

GIBB   Posted outside the town hall? / Was it?

LOUISE   You pushed / her down?

GIBB   A parish notice, was it? / An editorial?

LOUISE   Couldn't cope out here?

GIBB   You'd like that, would you, your most private, pinkest, tenderest – small bird, small bird, small fragile – stolen from you, slammed down onto the slab, the block, poked at and paraded. Butchered by a puppet, a dummy, a cartoon rapist.

LOUISE   Couldn't cope with her success? Eaten up with envy, was it? An act of violence? A miscalculation? A regrettable outburst? That's what they say.

GIBB   They.

LOUISE   Why are you still alive?

A child substitutes the shovel with another object. A plastic lobster, for example.

GIBB   How old you meant to be?

LOUISE   Who?

GIBB   Dressed like this.

LOUISE   When we first see her she's 33.

GIBB   You 33?

LOUISE   They age me. *(She calls.)* Sam.

GIBB   Ha.

LOUISE   The scene is when you first – When you first get together. '76. In the loft on West 10th. There's a glimpse of her on film on that night. Before she gets you home. She's by the window in a gallery. One of the few films we've got of her in the early days, before she

became who she was. She's talking to a man
– Perryman, we think – God, you should
know!

GIBB   I don't remember.

LOUISE   She's animated, angry even. It's a private
view. Her hair up. Pencil behind the ear. It's
when you meet. She looks like this. She takes
you back to the apartment. And we see her
on the film – and then she turns and walks
towards the door. She turns and walks. See?

LOUISE walks.

*This is the first time the fictional space is broken with a completed
physical action.*

GIBB   What do you want me to say?

LOUISE   It would be an honor, Margaret, if you
would just – just watch and be open. We
are having difficulties finding her. I have
undertaken a lot of work. Invested a lot of
time and energy. This is such a bonus to
have you – we didn't think – It would mean
a lot to me and to this film to – to have your
/ validation.

GIBB   Okay. Oh, I get it now. I think you have
made a profound mistake. Yes, a grave error,
an error of judgment.

LOUISE   Margaret.

GIBB   No help here. No help for me. No help for
you. No gift needed. Do not resuscitate.

What is this? Some kind of joke? Some trick
or treat? Dress up and scare me to death,
is it? Break my heart, is it? This pastiche.
This parody. This clown costume. This
embarrassment. Have you not, despite
your years, grown out of this? Oh, Christ,
now, if she were here she would mutilate
this – miscarriage – she would run you out
and down and off and you would not dare,
not dare to face me this way. Where's your
boyfriend?

LOUISE   He's not my boyfriend.

GIBB   Really? Bleeding his way around my house.
Snaffling around like a hog. My private
house. You cease this minute, you hear. You
cease and desist. I will not. What you have,
what you have here is some other person.
Some other person who is tired, who is just
tired. Who wishes to continue – unmolested.

Here, Boy.

GIBB walks away.

LOUISE   We're looking for the diaries.

GIBB walks back.

GIBB   You have no / right.

LOUISE   The notebooks, the journals she kept. She
didn't burn them right? She told Scott Berg
she would be buried with them – with them
and with other stuff. Is that right? Was that
just words?

GIBB   She spoke to no one.

LOUISE   What's out there?

GIBB   No one.

LOUISE   Is there a shallow grave? More work? You
                want to tell us where that is? The more you
                tell us, the sooner we'll be gone. There are
                plenty of people who would give a lot to see
                those papers. To understand the last years of
                her life. Her death. To stop the rumours. Not
                least the rumours about you.

                You don't come across as very nice,
                Margaret, not in this film. Not here. Not in
                real life.

GIBB   You don't know what happened.

LOUISE   We still have time to change the script, to
                rewrite the ending.

GIBB   Help. Rape. Rape. Take your hands off me.
                Take your / hands off.

LOUISE   Shut up. Shut up.

GIBB   You're nothing like her.

*A child executes a sequence of substitutions – ending with the 'spade' as
a pool noodle swim float, for example.*

*From this moment LOUISE's accent is naturalised southern Californian
with a hint of New Jersey.*

LOUISE   In three weeks we start to make a motion picture, do you understand that? Now, that's a fact of life, you can't change that – the green light is on – that's happening whether you want it to or not. When that movie is released, whether you help us or not, I will become your lover. To all the world, I will *become* her. I won't only be the actress who played her, I will *be* her. Be her. The real Janet is a long time dead and buried in the yard now, that's distant history now. When they think of Janet Adler, they will think of me. Now we could go ahead without you. Or you could help me get it right. It's your call.

GIBB   Who am I?

LOUISE   What?

GIBB   Who is me?

LOUISE   In the film?

GIBB   Do I even feature?

LOUISE   Oh. She's beautiful.

GIBB   I'm not beautiful.

LOUISE   You're a perfect match. She would love to meet you. We can fly you over. As a consultant or advisor. Or you could be in it. A walk-on, a cameo. We'd put you up

somewhere special. Get you out of this
place. Clean it up. Straighten it up. How
can you live in this chaos? This forest – this
vegetation – is that a tree, is that a real tree?
– how could you let this happen? This place
could be quite a place. See, you're warming
to the idea, hey, I can see it in your face.
Or you could come now – we have an RV,
a Winnebago. Whisk you away. The world
would love to see you. God you poor thing,
stuck here, building this wall around you. See
what happens when we take one brick away
from that wall. See how good that feels?
Margaret?

GIBB   What if we don't want to be remembered.

LOUISE   Everyone wants to be remembered.

GIBB   Is that so?

LOUISE   You made some of the most influential work
               of the late twentieth century.

GIBB   Not our intention.

LOUISE   Then you should have thought about that
               when you were doing it.

GIBB   How does it end?

LOUISE   The movie?

GIBB   What happens to me?

LOUISE   We want to tell the truth.

GIBB *(To the dog.)* Go to work.

The child/dog on stage 'attacks' LOUISE.

LOUISE clubs the child/dog to 'death' with whatever she's holding in her hand – the swim float, for example. A savage and playful struggle. The child twitches and eventually lies still.

STUDENT   In 1998, Adler & Gibb were invited
                to contribute a work to the Whitney's
                permanent collection. The artists considered
                the request and then told the museum that
                they would like to offer a new piece for
                them to acquire, rather than recommend
                an existing work. The work they presented
                was a three-month-old mongrel puppy.
                Isn't that cool? Um. In order to own the
                work, they said, the museum would need to
                commit to caring for, feeding, maintaining
                and protecting the dog. After much internal
                deliberation, the museum rejected their
                proposal, citing technical and administrative
                reasons.

                Slide.

A DOG is brought on to the stage by its owner. This dog should bear no necessary physical resemblance to any dog described in the text. It could be a different dog at every performance.

In 1992, during the first Gulf war, Adler
& Gibb organised a series of what they
famously termed 'un-events'. These took
the form of letting go – a request made to a
particular community to, and I quote, "open
all the doors, sanction the 'relaxed gaze', to
move at half pace, to speak at half voice. To
stop for fifteen minutes. To see to nature. To
record nothing of the moment but to let it
pass into forgetfulness, a collective release,
a pause between knowledge and action. An
intermission."

Wouldn't it be cool if we tried that now?

INTERVAL

The doors to the theatre are opened.

A relaxed affair – open and playful.

No one needs leave unless they want to.

The actors/children may stay on the stage.

The DOG will be petted.

Biscuits and squash and cups of tea for those on stage.

The set will be developed.

Trips to the bar/toilet for those in the audience.

The actor playing SAM will finesse the wound on his arm.

During the latter half of the interval, the children slowly start

to bring spades of earth or sand onto the downstage area

until it begins to form a barrow.

ACT TWO

As the STUDENT reads, the children continue to bring earth/sand onto the stage with plastic spades – downstage, away from the set which is nearing completion.

STUDENT

In an interview with *Artforum* in 1993 the critic Lucy Lippard described Adler's metamodern sensibility demonstrated in her *intermission* piece as existing "between hope and melancholy, between naïvety and knowingness, empathy and apathy, unity and plurality, totality and fragmentation, purity and ambiguity." So, how was that for you?

Look, I know you're busy people and I really appreciate your time for being here. I am grateful to the academy and the school board for their generosity and this opportunity to demonstrate – um – Okay. Sorry.

Slide, please.

LOUISE enters and watches the children at work.

Margaret Gibb delayed reporting her partner's death for three weeks. By that time her body was badly decomposed and the cause of her death could not be accurately established. Gibb was arrested for desecration but was never charged and, a year later, questions still hang above her involvement in Adler's death.

Slide, please.

As the STUDENT reads, SAM enters with a shovel of earth and joins in with the children. SAM's movements are laboured.

>Gibb fought to have her partner's body interred in the grounds of the house and her unmarked grave has become a place of pilgrimage for art lovers and students. The value of Adler's work – and her reputation – has risen considerably in the year since her death. Margaret Gibb has refused to give interviews – despite a continuing interest in her relationship with Adler.

>Slide, please.

The children keep 'building' the pile of earth – shaping and patting. They are simply playing on a sand pit as the scene plays out around them.

The performances are now three dimensional but not quite 'naturalised'.

SAM's accent is now from southern California, for example.

SAM and LOUISE stand either side of the grave. SAM with the shovel in his hand.

The children keep working.

The sound of a real forest plays – cicadas, etc.

LOUISE snorts a spoon of cocaine. 'Real' cocaine.

LOUISE   How do ya like *them* apples.

SAM vomits on to the stage. 'Real' vomit.

>Was there a marker?

SAM   No.

LOUISE   How did you find her?

SAM   The plants were a different colour – a deeper
                colour.

LOUISE   She'd appreciate that.

SAM   Like she fell asleep – curled up.

LOUISE   Tucked in.

SAM   Just beneath the surface.

LOUISE   Found you. Found you.

SAM   What now?

LOUISE   Give me the shovel.

SAM   There's still flesh on her.

LOUISE   It's earth.

SAM   Look.

LOUISE   They just wrapped her up.

SAM   Like an animal.

LOUISE   You seen any boxes?

SAM   Nothing.

LOUISE   Objects?

SAM   You'd think it would / have all gone.

LOUISE   A container, a – what do you call it? –

SAM   Ten years, you'd think it / would rot.

LOUISE   A capsule or –

SAM   I don't think we should –

LOUISE   It's earth.

SAM   She wanted it to rot, Lou. It's what she
            wanted.

LOUISE   Fuck it.

            Fuck.

SAM   I think we should clear out, you know, head
            back. I'm not feeling good. Really.

LOUISE   Yeah?

SAM   I don't think this is right. I think we've done
            enough.

LOUISE	You think?
SAM	How can you even question that? What the fuck, Louise, look what we're doing! We're digging up a fucking corpse. Put what we've got in the RV and head back.
LOUISE	Well I think we're in the middle of fucking nowhere and we are sitting on a gold mine here. I think we should control any ethical questions that we might be having at this moment in time, Sam, and keep looking. I think we should remember what is resting on this.
SAM	I know.
LOUISE	This is a big fucking deal.
SAM	I know.
LOUISE	So I think we should just put our personal considerations to one side just for a moment. You were happy enough to break a lock, smash a window / isn't that right?
SAM	We thought it was / empty.
LOUISE	And I think we should film this. Film her, Gibb – while she's still – Run a scene. The loft, maybe. The seduction. Capture it – with her. I'm ready for that now. I need that. My character needs that. The kiss and all. I think I can do that now. I think it's why we're here. For me. For my process. You're the one who said we should come. Have you forgotten that? You packed the tools. And then I

promise we will cover her up and we will pat her down and we will get the hell out of here and back to the dazzling civilization that is southern California.

SAM   I have to hand it to you, Louise, you know, I really – I thought you'd back out, you know. I thought you'd fail at the last – Can you believe this? Oh, man, we never thought it through! We never really thought it through.

LOUISE   No one will know.

The children continue in their work.

SAM   What's upstairs?

LOUISE   A second retrospective.

SAM   For real?

LOUISE   With the market like it is, you're kidding me.

SAM   What do you want to do?

LOUISE   Pick the whole house up and drop it in a hangar in Culver City. Adam considered that, you know.

Too bad about the sitting tenant.

SAM   Where is she?

LOUISE   Dealing with Lassie.

SAM   That was the dog, Lou.

LOUISE   What?

SAM   The Whitney dog.

LOUISE   The puppy?

SAM   Sixteen years now.

LOUISE   I killed it!

SAM   You killed it!

LOUISE   I killed it!

SAM   You killed it!

LOUISE   I killed the fucking art-dog!

SAM   You killed the art!

             Vincent van Dog.

LOUISE   Jackson Poodle. Pug-casso.

SAM   Husky Warhol.

LOUISE   She set it on me.

SAM   She could report what you did.

LOUISE	I feared for my life.
SAM	She has a gun.
LOUISE	So do we.
	In the flight case.
SAM	What does that mean?
LOUISE	It means we'll come back. We'll bring a truck.
SAM	This is not a movie here. We are not in a movie.
LOUISE	I'm not a retard.
SAM	There are consequences.
LOUISE	She's falling apart, Sam, look at this place.
SAM	She's tough as nails, Lou. Don't be deceived. She's like a fucking tree trunk. You saw her in there. You saw the look on her face.
LOUISE	She's a pussy cat.
SAM	She could eat us alive.
LOUISE	Only Adam knows we're here.
SAM	So?

LOUISE   It's a little late for re-writes, is all. The movie
                thinks Gibb is dead. Everyone thinks Gibb is
                dead. Even Gibb thinks Gibb is dead. If she
                won't help us, then let's leave it that way.

A child lies down supine on the mound of earth.

The other child hands SAM some 'real' vomit.

SAM vomits.

SAM   Holy Jesus.

LOUISE looks down at the child.

LOUISE   You got anything for me? Any surprises?

LOUISE touches the child's face.

SAM   Oh God, don't touch it!

LOUISE   I would wear her if I could.

SAM   I just came to help you work on your
                character.

LOUISE   And here she is. How many actors have this
                chance? Where's Hamlet's shallow grave?

67

What am I meant to do? Dress up and then walk away? Travel here and then just leave it? There are people who would go nuts for any kind of this – collectors around the world looking for / a piece –

SAM   It's her fucking home. This is her home. She has made a life here. It might not be your idea of a life, but it's a life. We can't come in and just – just assume.

LOUISE   Should we take something?

SAM   We've taken plenty.

LOUISE   No, here.

SAM   Like what?

LOUISE   I dunno. A bone?

SAM   What the fuck, Louise?

LOUISE   A finger. Not a fucking thigh, Jesus Christ. A finger. A finger.

SAM   You're kidding.

LOUISE   A lucky charm.

SAM   This is insane, completely fucking insane.

LOUISE	Look how the skull is coming away! Janet Adler's skull. This is an icon here, a relic. My character. My character.

The child fetches a skull and offers it to LOUISE.

SAM	Please don't.

LOUISE	I will wash my hands.

LOUISE takes the skull.

The child sits back down.

The abject.

Between the subject and the object! I studied this shit. What was I thinking? I am the artist. My character. I am the fucking artist now. I am. Get the camera.

SAM	I'm burning up, Lou.

LOUISE	Where are you now, hon, with your head full of earth? Where's your famous reticence now? Where's Buchenwald now, baby? Where's the West Village? Where's Andy fucking Warhol? I can't see him, can you? Nope, don't think you can. Where's your fascinating career, honey, your privacy, your principles, your spikey dykey lesbian schtick? Here they are, baby. Here they all are. You're looking at them.

Don't try to be interesting, darling.

69

(With the skull, Adler's accent coming in.) You're looking at me. I'm looking at you. You're looking at me. I'm looking at you. You're dead. (No fucking commentary!) I'm dead. You're dead. I'm dead. You're alive. I'm alive. You're alive. I'm alive. They kiss. Kiss kiss kiss.

SAM   There's your Golden Globe, there.

LOUISE   Isn't it, though.

What did she do to you? Come on. Tell me. You want me to get her for you?

SAM   Leave it.

LOUISE   That's the given circumstance, Sam. Just saying it. My super objective.

SAM   Not this.

LOUISE   Nothing you haven't taught me, Sam.

SAM   I didn't teach you this.

LOUISE   All you've ever said to me. All you have ever said – Understand the life of the character as a real person. This is the real person. The stakes have to be high, you say –

SAM   Pretty high right now, I'd say.

You're pretty high right now.

LOUISE   I am huge right now.

SAM   You have to breathe.

LOUISE   You have no idea right now how relaxed my
                fucking shoulders are.

She drops the skull.

                Stinks of hot hell.

                Gimme the wipes.

SAM   I'm out.

LOUISE   What?

SAM   I'm gonna wait in the RV.

LOUISE   You're going nowhere.

SAM   I'm poisoned.

LOUISE   Take an Advil.

SAM   This is not what I signed up for.

LOUISE   You stay here and you do as I say or you will
                never work again.

SAM   We broke in.

LOUISE   No one was hurt.

SAM   You killed the fucking dog.

LOUISE   This is the industry.

SAM   That's okay?

LOUISE   Thirty million dollars is okay.

SAM   You've confused the story.

LOUISE   I am the story.

SAM   For fuck's sake, Louise, I can't support this.

LOUISE   What do they say – you die twice – once
                when you die and again the last time
                your name is ever mentioned. We are the
                resurrection. We're bringing them back
                to life. We're the best thing that's ever
                happened to them.

Music plays – cinematic. Huge, swirling to start.

As the STUDENT speaks, SAM leads LOUISE through a series of acting exercises.

As the STUDENT speaks, the children complete the set.

As the STUDENT speaks, GIBB enters the setting.

As the STUDENT speaks the children leave the stage. Farewells.

STUDENT   The work of Janet Adler calls into question
                the, um, conventional strategies by which
                society preserves, cares for, and re-presents
                its culture. Her work was remarkable in
                its power of resistance towards the trend
                towards a cultural commodification.
                Um. As described by Lucy Lippard, it

was a de-emphasis on material aspects,
um, uniqueness, permanence, decorative
attractiveness, um, it lies in the non-material
realm of experience and interaction –
existing only for the moment of transmission
and prolonged within the memories of those
individuals who experienced it. A shift from
the perceptual to the conceptual, from the
physical to the mental, um.

Music stops.

Performances are 'realistic' now.

This is now, momentarily, a 'stage' play – being performed on a film set.

As the scene plays, SAM begins to prepare a camera set-up – camera, tripod, boom mic, portable lights, reflectors. He brings in a metal flight case. He is fading.

As SAM works, LOUISE undresses GIBB.

She will then dress her in a 'costume' – like a child dressing another child. The costume is mid-'70s Manhattan – ill-fitting.

She will apply make-up to her – like a child applying make-up to another child.

LOUISE   We got off to the wrong start, you and me,
           that's all. We got off on the wrong footing.
           I didn't express myself well. We weren't
           expecting to see you, that's all. I have a dog
           myself. I know how much they mean. They
           mean the world.

           Look at you, you poor thing. How could you
           let this happen? How could you let yourself

go like this? You lost all respect? I know how that feels, honey. You have to keep yourself together. Be true to yourself. Recognise your creativity. As a woman. Show the world who's boss!

GIBB   What is this?

LOUISE   We're dressing up, that's all! Never done that as a kid? This is fun! When did you last go upstairs? It's a treasure trove up there. Our designer would have a ball.

Slip this off.

LOUISE undresses GIBB – down to her underwear.

You have a good body for a woman your age. You've held yourself together. You're not old. What are you? Mid sixties? Seventy?

You had anything done or is it all God's bounty? I've had to give God's bounty a helping hand. You should have seen me when I was at college. Jesus! I was a mess! Flat-chested, naïve. Had to pull myself up. Run away. Take control. Like you! I credit you, you know, both of you, for how I turned out.

GIBB   Not so flat-chested.

LOUISE dresses GIBB.

LOUISE   Well, look at you!

I'm so pissed I missed the 70s. I love the 70s.
All that love and peace! Don't you wish it
was the 70s again.

GIBB   The work originally intended for this space
                has been withdrawn from sale.

LOUISE   I don't want to buy you, honey!

GIBB   The decision to withdraw has been taken as a
                protective measure.

LOUISE   I could fall in love with you all over again.

GIBB   A protective measure against the prevailing
                conditions.

LOUISE   You told us you were dead, remember?

GIBB   You hear me?

LOUISE   Never heard a dead woman speak, have we,
                Sam?

SAM   One minute.

GIBB   Are we heading for a repeat, is that it? Are
                we going to start again? Are we going to
                repeat the exact – what is it, moment? is it?
                – the exact gesture, is it? the tone of voice?
                Reproduce it? Remount it? What are you
                trying to hold on to here?

LOUISE	I always thought you were the pretty one.
GIBB	Is that what this is, all this? A teenage crush? A juvenile fantasy? You lost something, did you, along the way?
LOUISE	Always those eyes.
GIBB	You want these eyes again?
LOUISE	Blew me away those eyes, you did. Sam.
GIBB	We happened only once and you weren't there. You weren't there.
LOUISE	You know me? You seen my work?
	You seen any of my movies?
	Sam.
SAM	One minute.
LOUISE	Filming is a lot of waiting around.

SAM and LOUISE exit.

GIBB   She started to get confused a little, you know.
        A little out of sorts. She must have been just
        over 50 by then. I don't know dates. Mid
        '90s. I don't know. When we started to build
        this place. She started to forget where she put
        things, to have difficulty remembering words.
        This gave an interesting quality to the work.
        It also meant she was never satisfied. She was
        never satisfied anyway. Satisfied in us but not
        in the work.

        We were told there was no cure and she
        didn't want treatment anyway. There was no
        treatment. The diagnosis came as some kind
        of relief. Like saying goodbye to a problem
        she couldn't solve. We left and came here
        where I cared for her. We didn't make any
        announcements. All that was horseshit. We
        just left. We didn't have insurance and most
        of the work had gone by then. We didn't
        care. We hated the barbarians. We wanted
        out. We'd wanted out of it ever since we'd
        met, really. All the horseshit. This was our
        place. The work was ours. By the time she
        died, she didn't know the hand in front of
        her face. That's it.

        The last year of her was just cleaning,
        feeding and holding. Watching the yard and
        the creatures. Letting nature in. She was 70
        pounds at the end. The line between life and
        death was between the sea and the sky. She
        wanted to stay here and I wanted to stay with
        her. Let the nature in. I tried to join her, but I
        didn't have the nerve.

        Glamorous, murderous, action packed. Kind
        of thing you want to hear? I know what

77

people said about me. But none of that is
true. We just let the nature in. You want to
make a movie about that? 'cause that's the
story. About cleaning up the mess, is that
it, about changing the diapers, about things
falling apart, about holding someone till they
fade away?

When I dream of her it is always like you
were earlier. You got that bit right. The time
we met. In blue. The first night. The loft. I
would rather have her there – in my dream.

I would like to start again. I would like that.
But I know that isn't possible. I would like
to have it all again, but I know that isn't
possible. It is infantile to think otherwise.

If you kill me, which I think you should, you
put me with her, you hear me.

SAM hands GIBB a film script.

SAM   The scene is Scene 14. 14. Interior.
November '76. The loft apartment on West
10th. She's just found you. She's searched
for you after the opening and she's found
you. This is the night you first – you know –
Louise – the time you first – The seduction.
Janet wrote about it. The kiss. She wrote
about it. But we're having difficulties finding
it. Aren't we? Lou? Lou? Miss Mane is
feeling – blocked. This is the beginning of
your – Lou. Together, you and her. Tell us if

– And you tell us how it sounds, it feels, yes?
If it's real. And we film it. We –

LOUISE enters and takes her place on a mark in front of the film set.

Scene 14. Interior. When?

LOUISE   '76.

SAM   Precisely.

LOUISE   November '76.

SAM   Precisely.

LOUISE   November 12th '76.

SAM   What time is it?

LOUISE   1.30 a.m.

SAM   Temperature?

LOUISE   Mid-fifties. Overcast.

SAM   Cold?

LOUISE   No.

SAM   What then?

LOUISE   Margaret?

GIBB   –

LOUISE   I've been running. The walk up.

SAM	What are you wearing?
LOUISE	This.
SAM	Say it.
LOUISE	The blue blouse. Heavy cotton man's jacket. Pleated woolen skirt. Oxfords.
SAM	Tights or pantyhose?
LOUISE	Pantyhose.
SAM	What do you see?
LOUISE	Tiled wall.
SAM	Come on.
LOUISE	Margaret?

LOUISE looks around and describes the set exactly how it now is. The set that has been built by the children. She touches the things she describes. A literal description for the first time. Almost like a litany.

*However, at this moment, LOUISE, in the action of the play (in the derelict house, etc), is **imagining** these things – as part of an acting exercise to get her rooted in the 'reality' of the scene. She is imagining the elements of the Manhattan loft, when, for us, as the audience, the set and all these elements, are physically there. They have been built by the children in the course of play.*

Film score music starts to support this scene.

Papers, pictures, notes, sketches, etc *(For example – to be fixed when the set is finalised.)*

SAM   Detail.

LOUISE   Photos of woodland.

SAM   Detail.

LOUISE   Poster for a show.

SAM   What show?

LOUISE   I don't know.

SAM   Margaret?

LOUISE   Work with me.

SAM   I can't do this.

LOUISE   Coach me.

SAM   Say what you see.

LOUISE   I see the object of –

SAM   Simple.

LOUISE   I see a woman.

SAM   Keep it out.

LOUISE   She's looking at me.

SAM   She's looking at –

LOUISE   You're looking at me.

SAM   Now you say – you say –

LOUISE   Say what you see. You say it now, say what
               you see.

GIBB   I don't recognize myself.

LOUISE   I'm looking at you.

GIBB   I don't know this.

LOUISE   Sam.

SAM   *(To GIBB.)* Here's the deal. Here's what we
               do. Listen. All of you listen. Listen. Here's
               how we do it. Here's how we find – There is
               a system of wants. You understand? Truth.
               Commitment. Authenticity. You understand?
               This is the – Of wants. What do you want?
               What does your character want? Yes? We
               are doing the research. There isn't this and –
               something else. There isn't this and then this.
               It's life. The work is life. Life is the work. All
               this. This work. This is not a game. We are
               not playing. Look. We find the mindset of the
               task. A task is the objective, is the character's
               desire transformed into something that is
               achievable in the real world. That's what it is.
               And in this instance we know the real world.
               We are in the real world. The obstacle –
               What do you want to achieve? What do you
               want? Your object. What is your – What do
               you want? And how are you going it get it?
               Who are you and what do you want? That's
               all there is – This is your – your – This is all
               there is. ALL. Object, obstacle, intention.
               You enter the scene. The scene is here.
               You enter the scene. You and you. You are

thinking – there – there. You enter the scene.
What do you want? You are looking. What is
your obstacle? Nothing you do is not driven.
Nothing. How are you going to overcome
your – And get what you want? There. Yes.
There. Yes. Here. That's all there is. Your
character. Your – It's late. The external –
your – the – We have done this. We have
done this. And you, you USE the work, the
work, to get deeper, to get what you want.
You want. You get what you want. You are
here. You are here. Do it. Do it. I can't. I
can't.

SAM dies.

*As the STUDENT reads, a member of the stage crew brings on a screen
(a monitor) and connects the camera to it.*

*As the STUDENT reads, a member of the stage crew helps SAM up, hands
him a towel and takes him off stage.*

*As the STUDENT reads the camera is switched on – and the feed goes
to the monitor.*

*The camera is set up so everything that needs to be is in frame. The frame
reads as a Manhattan loft apartment from the 1970s. The apartment
where Adler & Gibb got together.*

*As the STUDENT reads, Adler & Gibb take up position in front of the
camera – in frame.*

STUDENT   In one real sense, we could read the death
                  of Janet Adler – her non-existence – as her
                  last work of art – her insistence on non-

temporality. Even though the original media of the work (the artist herself) has become obsolete (dead!), processes of emulation and reproduction can help support our understanding of the work using the metaphoric value of the outdated medium (the artist!) – even if that medium no longer exists!

The work of Janet Adler questions notions of permanence – particularly when we consider the last years of her life and the clues that may exist in the facts of her death when they are finally uncovered. It is the responsibility of future generations to keep the memory of Adler's output alive so that her influence can be understood and her symbolic importance preserved.

The scene plays out through the onstage camera and is fed onto a screen. The voices are amplified by the boom mic.

The scene is underscored by music and the sound of Manhattan.

INT. APARTMENT – NIGHT

ADLER
Aren't you hot?

GIBB
This is a wonderland.

ADLER
You are a wonderland.

GIBB
I saw you looking.

ADLER

This evening, I could see nothing else. The
sight of you took the breath from my lungs.
Oh, darling, if you only knew. Oh, honey.
Don't you feel it, do you? It will all end
with us, you know, with only us. You and
me. You know that too, don't you? We will
be like climbing partners roped together.
If one of us goes, then they will pull
the other with them. Gladly down into the
crevasse.

GIBB

Your voice is heat. Your words are light.

ADLER

The blood rushes to all those parts of the
body and I am light-headed.

GIBB

I should go home.

ADLER

You are home.

GIBB

Really?

ADLER

Don't you feel it? Your journeys are over.

THEY KISS.

The kiss sustains.

The music sustains and begins to turn violent and chaotic.

The STUDENT reads.

As the STUDENT reads, the kiss moves out of frame and onto the floor.

The kiss is real. Clothes are removed.

As the STUDENT reads, the kiss becomes violent.

It's indistinct by this time, but the suggestion is that LOUISE might kill GIBB. There is a small metal flight case. A gun shot, maybe.

The music becomes deafening, crashing.

STUDENT   The questions surrounding the life and
               death of Janet Adler highlight the need
               to record, archive, document and classify
               contemporary culture in its multiplicity of
               forms. Contemporary art challenges the
               underlying values of conservation and new
               forms of preservation must be found to keep
               pace with an ever-changing culture. Um.

               I never had the opportunity to meet Ms
               Adler, but I know that she has had a
               profound impact on me – and, um, on my –

The STUDENT's speech is drowned out by the music.

The actors leave the stage.

A film is projected on a large screen.

The film is underscored.

The film presents many of the things we have only been able to see in our mind's eye. The inside of a Winnebago. A house. A forest. The roots of a tree. A fence. A gate. A broken lock. An old photo of a house. A deer. A

*handgun. An angle grinder. A disturbed shallow grave. Etc. Maybe the
sense of a corpse – either SAM's or GIBB's – or both.*

The film ends.

LOUISE enters in award-ceremony attire.

Music and rapturous applause.

She goes to the lectern.

LOUISE   This is the consummation of a long love
                affair! Oh, boy, you don't know! Seriously,
                thank you. Thank you!

                When I was, um, when I was a kid, my mom
                – my mom who is here tonight! – my mom
                met Miss Adler in a diner in New York City
                and Miss Adler signed a napkin she had
                sketched on and she gave it to my mom and
                my mom brought it home and showed it to
                me and that, I guess, was the beginning of
                this incredible journey! The start of my love
                affair with the life and work of an artist who
                would come to mean so much to me – to
                women around the world and to us all! And I
                still have that napkin, can you believe!

LOUISE presents a Ziplock bag with a napkin in it. Applause.

                This is my connection! I cannot begin to
                tell you what it means to me to be able to
                stand here today and honor the story of a
                woman, a woman who touched so many
                lives through her bravery, her artistry and

her unwillingness to compromise. This is for you, Janet Adler. You made me want to be the best actor that, I guess, I never knew I could be!

Oh, god! I want to thank everyone I have ever met! The Academy, Stacey, Peter and Eddie at Viacom, Sandy, Keith – this film was such fun to make! – and my darling husband, Adam – where are you, Adam? – without you none of this would have been possible!

Oh! I won't cry. I promised myself I wouldn't cry.

I love the world! I'm so happy! Thank you.

Rapturous applause. Music swells.

END

what happens to the hope
at the end of the evening

to the memory of Adrian Howells.

what happens to the hope at the end of the evening written and performed by Tim Crouch & Andy Smith

Directed by Karl James

An Almeida Festival commission supported by Live at LICA

First performance at the Almeida Theatre on July 9th, 2013

At the Almeida, the part of Andy was shared between Andy Smith and Sue Maclaine

Thanks:

Sue Maclaine, Maja Bugge, Holly Smith, Nel Crouch, Matt Fenton and LICA, Alice Booth, Jennifer Gaskell, Cathy Chapman, Lisa Wolfe, Lucy Morrison, Dawn Taylor, Aggi Agostino and everyone at the Almeida.

The lay-out of the play is a facsimile of the text
as used in performance.

what happens to the hope at the end of the evening

Tim Crouch & Andy Smith

**** appears in the script as an indicator of a break or a 'time warp',
but is not always indicative of a pause, silence or space. It
suggests – amongst other things – a moment of 'making strange',
a moment like a jump cut in a film, or even (for ANDY) just a shift
of position in his chair.*

*Where page turns are not noted the dialogue should carry on,
happily accepting the act of turning the page as part of the scene.*

---

*To one side of the stage, a chair and a music stand
holding this script.*

*A general cover of light on the stage. Gentle houselights
on the audience.*

*ANDY and FRIEND enter from the same door as the
audience. ANDY carries a water bottle.*

The FRIEND takes a place centre stage.

*ANDY sits down on the chair and takes off his shoes. He
prepares to start.*

ANDY and the FRIEND look at each other.

ANDY looks to the audience and turns the page.

ANDY   Right then.

            (*To the front of house manager.*) Karl (*eg.*),
            is everyone here who said they were
            coming? Great.

            Thanks, everyone.
            Here we are.

            I don't know about you, but this… this is
            one of my favourite things to do in the
            whole world. Just being together with
            some people in a room like this. A space
            like this, you know? A space where we
            can really be together, sit together and
            listen to a story.

            It's a Saturday night in Lancaster, a small
            city in the North-West of England.
            Surrounded by beautiful countryside, it
            faces west across Morecambe Bay and out
            towards the South Lakes.

It's early summer. The warmth of the day can still be felt in the limestone walls of the houses that surround a public square.

One of those houses is my house. Above the front door there is a Sanskrit inscription. A mantra that evokes blessings that arise at times of enlightenment.

It's 9pm.

And I am waiting. I'm waiting for my friend. I haven't seen him for a long time.

A space.

ANDY turns the page.

***

ANDY   I remember one time, a few years ago, just
              for something to do, I took my friend to a
              church service. We sat at the back and
              tried not to giggle. We'd been up all night,
              I think.

              It was a very calming experience. We
              listened to the hymns and the readings and
              the sermon, and then we got to the bit
              where the congregation is asked to
              exchange the sign of peace. You know,
              when you shake each other's hand and
              say 'Peace be with you'. Well, my friend
              misheard it! Rather than saying, 'Peace be
              with you', he shook everyone's hand and
              said 'pleased to meet you'. Pleased to
              meet you! I thought that was rather nice.

              Why don't we do it now? While we wait.
              Just turn to the people nearest to you,
              shake their hand and say 'pleased to meet
              you'.

ANDY gently encourages the audience to do the same,
stepping down into the auditorium and shaking hands with
the members of the audience sitting nearest to him.
He returns to his position on the stage.

Thanks, everyone.

ANDY sits down, and prepares himself.
ANDY looks at the FRIEND.

ANDY   Alright, mate.

***

FRIEND   Fuck, mate, I thought you were dead!

ANDY   Did you?

FRIEND   Not really dead, mate, not dead really. But
             do you ever get that, though, when you
             haven't seen or heard from someone for a

long time and when you think about them you think they might be dead or paralysed or totally unrecognisable for all you know because it's been such a long time, even though it might only have been a year, and then you see them after thinking that and they look just like they did when you saw them last? You can't comprehend that they've just been getting on with their lives like you've just been getting on with yours. But because you haven't spoken to them or thought about them then it's like they're dead, or dead to you even though they're alive in their own - you know - lives. And it feels weird because you think that time must have had some effect on them – or that being away from you must have had some effect on them - but it doesn't seem to have done. And you think it's probably the same for them - they think the same about you?

Do you ever get that?

ANDY   I tell him: I'm very much alive, mate.

FRIEND	I thought you'd moved or changed your email or gone back to Norway or just that I'd totally fucking offended you in some totally heinous fucking mortal way or that you just hated my guts and never wanted to see me again! Or something had happened, mate, at least. Has something happened? Mate, has it? Are you okay?
ANDY	I'm fine. We're fine.
FRIEND	You haven't posted anything for over a year, for fuck's sake! Your profile picture is still the same! Seriously, though, mate, it's good to hear your voice. Are you okay? How's life? How's Maja? How's Molly? How old is she now, mate?
ANDY	Nearly four, mate.
FRIEND	Fucks sake! I've left you loads of messages.
ANDY	Mate, it's not personal. You know what it's like. Life slips through your fingers. It's great to hear from you, mate. What are you phoning for?

ANDY looks at the FRIEND. A space. ANDY turns the page.

***

The French philosopher Alain Badiou suggests that love is 'a successful struggle against separation'.

Relating this idea to the processes of theatre, he considers 'the moment of great melancholy', when the people involved in performing and staging break up. When numbers are exchanged knowing that no-one will call.

I'm waiting for my friend, my old friend. He said he would be here by now.

***

FRIEND   I'm coming up to Manchester and thought I could just pop over.

ANDY   That would be great.

FRIEND   Yeah?

ANDY   I tell him I need to check with Maja.

FRIEND	Oh, don't worry about it. It was just a thought.
ANDY	Mate, I would love it.
FRIEND	No, no, no, mate, wouldn't dream of it, you need to check with Maja.
ANDY	That's not what I mean.
FRIEND	Just to crash.
ANDY	I ask him when.
FRIEND	Weekend after next. The 28th. Just for the night.
ANDY	I tell him, that's perfect. Molly and Maja are in Oslo then. I say: I'd love to see you, mate.
FRIEND	You sure?
ANDY	Absolutely.
FRIEND	Yeah?
ANDY	When do you think you'd be getting here?
FRIEND	Seven?
ANDY	Are you driving?
FRIEND	Train.
ANDY	I'll pick you up from the station.
FRIEND	Don't worry about it, I'll walk up. I'll enjoy the walk.

ANDY	I'll cook.
FRIEND	I can pick something up on the way.
ANDY	I'm happy to cook.
FRIEND	I'll bring a bottle, then.
ANDY	You don't need to.
FRIEND	You still in the same place?
ANDY	I ask him: what are you up to in Manchester?
FRIEND	There's an anti-fascist thing in Bolton.
ANDY	Yeah?
FRIEND	Yeah. The EDL are planning a sort of quaint little reconstruction of Kristallnacht on the Chorley Road, like the Sealed Knot, a historical reenactment – with mosques instead of synagogues. There's a bunch of us coming up from London. It was in the newsletter. Do you still get the newsletter? Are you still on the list?
ANDY	No.
FRIEND	We thought we'd come and say hello to the racists, you know, a little welcome party, show them the error of their ways. Like old times, remember?

ANDY	How could I forget?
FRIEND	You should come.
ANDY	It's a busy time.
FRIEND	Molly and Maja are away, you said, what's your excuse?

A short space. ANDY turns the page.

***

ANDY   My friend and I used to share a tiny flat on the North End Road, but then I met Maja and I moved to Norway.

ANDY looks at the FRIEND. The FRIEND exits. ANDY looks back to the audience.

Maja is Norwegian. We wanted to be together, so I went there and started making work like this.

I needed a change, you know? It felt like a shift needed to happen. And it was really liberating. Almost like becoming a new person.

We came back not long after Molly was born, when I got offered the opportunity to do a PhD in theatre at Lancaster University. It's so much cheaper to live in the North. There's so much more space.

A space.

The FRIEND enters - with bag, wine bottle, coat, flowers, etc.

***

ANDY   I'm waiting for my friend. He can't be far
              away. I thought I saw him. Or someone
              like him. Outside my house. Standing on
              the front steps.

                              ***

FRIEND   Fuck, mate, Andy, come see this, look.
              The most beautiful evening.

ANDY   Yes. It's great, isn't it? Come inside.

FRIEND   The sky's almost violet. You should come
              see this.

ANDY   Yes. The skies are great here.

FRIEND   But this one.

ANDY   You're here now.

ANDY turns the page.

FRIEND   Come and see.

ANDY   I'm okay, mate, really.

                  It's good to see you.

FRIEND   I fucking love this stillness. Don't you?

                  Doesn't matter if it's cold or overcast or – I

                  fucking love it when it's still.

ANDY   Yes.

                  Nice, mate.

FRIEND   Thanks, mate.

ANDY   Come inside, mate. Take your shoes off.

                  Dump your stuff.

FRIEND   I saw a fox on the way up here. We looked

                  at each other between two parked cars.

                  As far away as you are now.

ANDY   Are you okay?

***

14

FRIEND	Who's that kid?
ANDY	What?
FRIEND	There's a kid, standing by the edge of the green.
ANDY	Yeah?
FRIEND	Yeah. He's looking over here. Watching us.
ANDY	Come inside.

The FRIEND 'engages' with the kid.

***

ANDY	My friend is here.
	I'm waiting for my friend.

ANDY turns the page.

ANDY   I wonder what might happen here this
            evening. I wonder what could happen, you
            know? What could we do here? These are
            the moments that I find exciting. The
            moments when it feels as if there isn't
            anything to distract us. The moments when
            everything goes quiet.

            Like this.

*The FRIEND puts down the bottle and flowers and drags
on a coffee table. Places objects on the table - magazines,
a candle, etc. He brings on a sofa and other things - to
make a 'setting'. A laborious process done with great
attention to detail.*

                        ***

FRIEND   Your place is looking great, mate.
ANDY   Thanks.
FRIEND   It's such a great place.
ANDY   Yes.

FRIEND	Really together.
ANDY	Thanks.
FRIEND	Must be worth a few quid now.
ANDY	We could do with a bit more room.
FRIEND	Have you done something to it?
ANDY	Took out a wall, mate.
FRIEND	Fuck, yeah, yeah! It's great.
ANDY	Thanks.

FRIEND	Come and sit down.
ANDY	You hungry?
FRIEND	Later, maybe.
ANDY	It's pretty late now, mate.
FRIEND	Yeah, sorry, sorry.

ANDY	How were the fascists?
FRIEND	The EDL or the police?
ANDY	Do you make a distinction?

ANDY turns the page.

FRIEND	God, when did I see you last?
ANDY	Your wedding.
FRIEND	Shit, that was two years ago.
ANDY	Yes.
FRIEND	Yeah. Fuck. Sorry, sorry.
ANDY	We've both been busy.
FRIEND	It's beautiful though. Beautiful view.
ANDY	Your place is nice, I seem to remember.
FRIEND	Yeah.
ANDY	In Balham, was it?
FRIEND	Peckham. I'm not there at the moment.
ANDY	Yeah?
FRIEND	Still paying half the rent, though, until we sort something out.
ANDY	Oh, mate, really?
FRIEND	Yeah, yeah.
ANDY	So soon.
FRIEND	What's that supposed to mean?
ANDY	Your marriage, I mean.
FRIEND	You don't plan these things, mate.
ANDY	Mate.

FRIEND	I seem to be emotionally incontinent, that's the phrase that's being flung at me. Better than being incontinent incontinent, I suppose. Fewer wet patches, or wet patches of a far sexier nature.
ANDY	Are you okay?
FRIEND	Not really
ANDY	You're shaking, mate.
FRIEND	Fuck it.
ANDY	What's wrong?
FRIEND	Just coming in to this heat, mate. Your house is hot, man. Could we open a window?
ANDY	What's been happening?
FRIEND	Why is it so fucking hot?
ANDY	It doesn't feel too bad for me, mate.
FRIEND	Well, it's hot.
ANDY	I suggest that he takes his coat off.

A space.

ANDY looks at the FRIEND.

Take your coat off, mate.

***

The FRIEND takes his coat off during the following speech

ANDY   I am waiting for my friend. My friend of
              nearly 30 years. I think about all the things
              that we have done. I think about how, as
              young men, we moved through the world
              together. How we pushed and shoved.
              I think about everything that has happened
              since. About everything that has been said
              and not said. And now here we are.

                         ***

FRIEND   Can I have some of your water?
ANDY   Yeah.

ANDY hands the FRIEND his bottle of water.
The FRIEND takes a drink, then pours it over himself.

FRIEND   Fuck! That's better.
ANDY   Steady, mate.
FRIEND   Sorry, sorry, etc.

	Come and be with me.
ANDY	I'm okay here, mate.
FRIEND	Are you pissed off?
ANDY	No.
FRIEND	You sulking?
ANDY	No.
FRIEND	Do you want me to go and get you some more water?
ANDY	If I want some I can go and get some.
FRIEND	From the kitchen?
ANDY	What?
FRIEND	If you went to get some more water would you go into the kitchen to get it?
ANDY	All right.
FRIEND	The kitchen?
ANDY	The kitchen.
FRIEND	The kitchen?
ANDY	Do you want me to say yes?
FRIEND	The kitchen.
ANDY	Yes.

ANDY turns the page.

FRIEND	You sure?
ANDY	If you want.
FRIEND	Not if I want. It's what you want.
ANDY	Yes.
FRIEND	Where exactly is your kitchen, mate, I've forgotten? Is it through there?
ANDY	If you want.
FRIEND	What did I say?
ANDY	Sorry.
FRIEND	You want me to go into the kitchen?
ANDY	No.
FRIEND	I can get you some now.
ANDY	I've been waiting for you.
FRIEND	Let me go get some.
ANDY	No.
FRIEND	Mate!

***

	I'm sorry mate, I'm just twatting around. It's so good to see you, Andy. So good. Here give us a hug. You haven't given us a hug yet.
ANDY	Mate, you're soaked.
FRIEND	It's only water.
ANDY	I'd rather not get wet.
FRIEND	Fuck's sake, mate, it's just water.
ANDY	I'd rather not.
FRIEND	Come on!
ANDY	I'll be wet for the rest of the evening.
FRIEND	You'll dry out.

ANDY turns the page.

ANDY   In her 2009 book 'Theatre & Audience',
             Helen Freshwater writes the following:
             'Our sense of the proper, or ideal
             relationship between theatre and its
             audiences can illuminate our hopes for
             other models of social interaction'.
             She suggests that the theatre is a place in
             which we can clarify thought around some
             of our expectations of community, of
             democracy, of citizenship.

They hug. They play.

They sit back down.

FRIEND   Come and sit down on the sofa.
ANDY   I'm happy here, thanks.

                         ***

FRIEND   You've put on weight.

ANDY   Yeah?

FRIEND   Yeah.

ANDY   You're completely bald now.

FRIEND	Is this a competition?
ANDY	I think so.
FRIEND	You've gone grey. Specially in your beard.
ANDY	You've got glasses.

FRIEND	They're really only for reading, but I think they make me look sexy.
ANDY	They do, mate. Really sexy.

	You're looking good.
FRIEND	Thanks, mate. So are you.
ANDY	Thanks.
FRIEND	Come and join me.

ANDY	How *is* your marriage, mate?
FRIEND	How's yours?
ANDY	I asked first.
FRIEND	You look stressed.
ANDY	Is this still the competition?
FRIEND	I'm just saying.
ANDY	I've got lots on.

ANDY turns the page.

FRIEND	Marking essays?
ANDY	I'm really fine.
FRIEND	You look tired.
ANDY	Maybe I don't get as much sleep as I used to.
FRIEND	Yeah?
ANDY	No parent does.
FRIEND	No?
ANDY	Sometimes Molly comes in.
FRIEND	Into your bed?
ANDY	We like it.
FRIEND	Fuck's sake, she's nearly four.
ANDY	We like it.
FRIEND	Your choice, mate.
ANDY	I'm not complaining.
FRIEND	Sounds like it.
ANDY	My life is great, mate.
FRIEND	You win.

	Fuck, we're not getting any younger!
ANDY	That's it.

***

The FRIEND opens a bottle, pours and drinks a glass of wine, and pours another before ANDY begins to speak. Over the course of the following exchanges the FRIEND drinks several glasses.

ANDY   I'm looking forward to seeing my friend. I can't remember the last time we managed to sit down and have a real conversation. A conversation about all that is wrong with the world, and how we might set it all to rights.

***

FRIEND   And nobody's really all that bothered. Not really. Not even the racists who just want to be in a pub watching football. You listening, Andy?

ANDY   Yes.

ANDY turns the page.

FRIEND   Then the Greater Manchester Police decide to have a party - break things up. They were breaking up anyway, you know. We were all about to go home. The fucking cops start closing in on us – on us! Not the white supremacists. Not the fucking Nazis. And we have every right to be there, so we start pushing back. This is not a riot, Andy. We are doing nothing wrong. And the fucking horses are brought in. We are peaceful, Andy, you know me, this is a peaceful action. But when you have a horse towering over you, with some twat of a copper shouting at you to move back, well -

ANDY   Yes.

FRIEND   But I had every right to be there, you know. And I'm doing nothing except protesting peacefully when a load of them try to separate us from the main group and before I know it, I've fallen off the kerb and there are three fucking coppers all over me. And I did nothing, mate. Nothing. They bundle me like I'm some fucking danger to society. I'm nearly fifty! They rip my fucking jacket. And I'm calling for some decent fucking human rights and Lucy from the Alliance is laying into them. Do your remember her, Andy? Well they nearly cuff her. And the fuckers threaten to charge me for public affray – like I'm some piss head on a Saturday night.

ANDY   Yes.

FRIEND   You should have been there. You'd feel better about yourself.

ANDY   Yes.

FRIEND   And then the obligatory pint and then Lucy walks me to the station and here I am. Fuck mate sorry I'm so late. I've brought you these.

The FRIEND offers ANDY the flowers

ANDY   Is it Lucy?

                        ***

I am waiting for my friend. I worry that something might have happened.

ANDY turns the page.

***

The FRIEND destroys the flowers.

***

ANDY   Our house is ex-council. It's made of
              limestone and sits on a public square with
              a green in the middle. It's in a good part of
              town and feels like a real community.

              We are happy in this place. The
              neighbours are friendly. One day a year
              the residents move their furniture outside
              and we all get to know each other. We
              share food and drink. We hang fairy lights
              in the trees. We watch the sun set.

***

FRIEND   He's still there.

ANDY   Who?

FRIEND   That kid. With his mates now.

ANDY	Yes.
FRIEND	They're just watching us.
ANDY	Yes.
FRIEND	Come and see.
ANDY	No.
FRIEND	It's getting dark.
ANDY	Yes.
FRIEND	Shouldn't they be at home?
ANDY	It's fine.
FRIEND	What are they doing?
ANDY	Nothing.
FRIEND	They're looking at us.
ANDY	Yes.
FRIEND	I should go out and have a word.
ANDY	Leave it, mate.
FRIEND	Should I draw the curtains?
ANDY	It's fine.
FRIEND	It's like being in a goldfish bowl.
ANDY	Is it a problem?
FRIEND	People staring in.
ANDY	I don't think it's a threat.

ANDY turns the page.

***

ANDY   It's good to see you.

FRIEND   Can I smoke in here?

ANDY   I'd rather you didn't.

FRIEND   I'll open the window.

ANDY   I'd rather you didn't.

FRIEND   I'll sit by the fireplace and blow it up the chimney.

ANDY   I'd rather you didn't, mate.

FRIEND   Fuck's sake, mate, just the one.

ANDY   Maja will smell it.

FRIEND   You're joking.

ANDY   She'll smell it.

FRIEND   Mate, she's not back till Monday. How the fuck would she smell one cigarette, smoked out the window - when she's not coming back till Monday!

ANDY   She'll smell it.

FRIEND   Is she superhuman? Does she have a superhuman nose?

ANDY   You can when you're pregnant.

FRIEND   You never told me.

ANDY   I don't see you.

FRIEND   Fuck's sake, mate.

ANDY   I wanted to see you.

FRIEND   When's it due?

ANDY   End of next month.

FRIEND   That's fucking amazing.

ANDY   Thanks.

FRIEND   We should have a cigar.

ANDY   I tell him he can smoke out on the front step.

FRIEND   Seriously?

ANDY   I tell him to make sure he stubs it out on the wall, check that it's not hot, and then drop it in the bin.

FRIEND   Fuck's sake.

The FRIEND pours a glass of wine and drinks it.

ANDY turns the page.

***

ANDY   Living in Norway had a really big influence
              on me. Learning a new language,
              experiencing a new culture. It felt like it
              really freed me up to explore what I really
              wanted to do, you know?

              It was just after we started a family that we
              decided that we wanted to come back to
              the UK. The PhD felt like a good
              opportunity to consolidate some thoughts,
              you know? To think and write around what
              the theatre does, and what it might be able
              to do.

A space.

                         ***

ANDY   Before you come back in, can you take
              your shoes off?

FRIEND   That's not me.

ANDY   What?

FRIEND   That shit smell.

ANDY   I can't smell any shit.

FRIEND	There's certainly shit, mate, but it's not me.
ANDY	Your shoes, mate.
FRIEND	They're clean, mate. It's not me.
ANDY	It's not about that.
FRIEND	Mate, they're totally clean, look. There is no shit on my shoes. Look. Look. It must be your shoes. You've brought some shit in. There's shit all over the place out there – on the walk up, on the verge, the pavement just outside your house there's some. It's like a big dog shithole. I fucking hate it, don't you, when people don't clear up after their dogs. The closest I've come to thumping someone recently was some dick I watched drive up to the small park near us, let his dog out, watch it shit on the grass and then call it back to the car. I said, excuse me, mate, do you live round here? He said, no. I said, well I fucking do and I don't come round to where you live and shit in your place, do I, so clean up your fucking dog's mess. He said he was going to leave me to do it, then locked his car and started to drive off. I fucking smacked my fist on his bonnet and he

stopped and got out and we started this fucking shouting match. I've never felt so angry. I could have killed him.

ANDY   Did he clear it up?

FRIEND   Have a look at your shoes. It'll be your shoes.

ANDY   Mate, there isn't any shit. It's not about or anything to do with shit.

FRIEND   What's it about then?

ANDY   It's just what we do. It's a Norwegian thing. We take our shoes off when we come in.

FRIEND   Nice.

ANDY   It shows you've arrived at a place. Shows you're really here.

FRIEND   Shows you've spent some money on a new carpet.

ANDY   I like it.

FRIEND   No, I like it.

ANDY   Shows some respect, that's all. It's a respectful thing to do. It's relaxing. And it helps your feet to breathe. You could do it if you want. Why don't we all take our shoes off? Wouldn't it be lovely if we all took our shoes off?

ANDY encourages the audience to take off their shoes.
The FRIEND sits on the sofa and takes off his shoes. He
fetches a glass of wine and sits back down on the sofa.

Thanks, everyone.

Here we are.

My research is all about things like this. I
have been thinking about what happens
here and what can happen here. Thinking
about what we are doing here. Thinking
about what we might do from here.

The FRIEND gets up and stands next to ANDY.

***

I am waiting for my friend.

At least you got here on time.

***

ANDY turns the page.

FRIEND	There's a group of them now.
ANDY	Yes.
FRIEND	On your 'village green'.
ANDY	Yes.
FRIEND	Like a gang.
ANDY	Yes.
FRIEND	Looks like something's kicking off.
ANDY	They're just kids.
FRIEND	Look older than just kids. Looks like something's being organized.
ANDY	Maybe it is.
FRIEND	Looks like they're going to start something.
ANDY	It's fine. They're at a loose end, but it isn't a problem. This is a good neighbourhood.
FRIEND	When I walked up here from the station, it didn't look like a good neighbourhood.
ANDY	No?
FRIEND	No, it looks like a shithole, mate. It's Saturday night and there was no one around. The shops are all shuttered. The boozers were empty.
ANDY	It's a difficult time.
FRIEND	Then don't tell me it's not a problem, Andy.

Line.

ANDY   "Look at them, Andy. Young kids with nothing to do."

FRIEND   Look at them, Andy. White kids with fuck all to do.

ANDY   Mate.

FRIEND   What kind of a fucking future do they have? These are the dispossessed, Andy. They've been abandoned by the very people who are meant to be looking after them. Every policy of this government chips away at their future. How can you sit there and watch that, you know? They need help. From people like you. No wonder they're furious. I'd have a go if I were them.

ANDY   I think that being here has the potential to be radical. I think it could be radical. I think these are the spaces where we can see where we are. Where we can think about where we might be going.

ANDY turns the page.

The FRIEND drags the sofa nearer to ANDY and fetches a glass of wine. While he does this ANDY continues to speak the following.

I think these places might be one of the few places left where we can just get together and sit quietly for an hour or so. And I don't think we should be afraid to do something like that.

A space.

***

I am waiting for my friend.

FRIEND   And you're suggesting that I scrunch up my eyes and it goes away?

ANDY   You could try that.

FRIEND   I don't just wang it around, mate.

ANDY   You say it's uncontrollable.

FRIEND   Fuck's sake. I'm saying it's not like fucking Tourettes, aren't I? It's not a tic. It's not just an itch that will go away if I leave it alone.

ANDY   You asked me what I do.

FRIEND	Fuck sake, Andy. We're animals, you know. We only started thinking 40,000 years ago. It's a relatively new thing for us.
ANDY	So, did you fuck her, then, Lucy?
FRIEND	Why do you think I went to Bolton?
ANDY	Lucy from the Alliance.
FRIEND	Juicy Lucy.
ANDY	Where is she now?
FRIEND	With her husband.
ANDY	Is she still with Adrian?
FRIEND	Yeah.
ANDY	Jesus.
FRIEND	It is fucked. I am fucked.

ANDY turns the page.

***

ANDY   I tell him not to see her again.

FRIEND   It's all so fucking easy for you. You don't
              get caught up in it. Not everyone does a
              bit of yoga, has a little think, gets their
              organic veg box, has a little think, loves
              their mum and dad, has a little think -

ANDY   Well, maybe they should!

              Maybe it's that simple, you know? Don't
              fuck that person who isn't your partner.
              Don't open that third bottle of wine. Don't
              make assumptions. You talk as if these
              things are out of our control, well maybe
              they are not.

              Look at us. Maybe we just need to stop
              and think for a minute. Maybe we can
              become better people just by living better
              lives. Or at least by trying to live a better
              life. But I think we need to think about
              what that really means. And try to really
              work out what it might take. I don't know if I
              think we know anymore. I don't know if we
              know what we want anymore.

FRIEND   Right now, I know I want to become a better person by kicking your fucking face in.

The FRIEND finishes the bottle of wine.

I'm going to get some more booze, you want anything?

The FRIEND puts on his shoes and jacket. He exits.

***

A space

ANDY   I don't know if there are many other places where I think we might be able to connect like this. Really connect.

ANDY turns the page. The FRIEND comes in quick here!

***

43

The FRIEND enters with a new bottle of wine.

FRIEND   They were blocking my way.

ANDY   Who?

FRIEND   The kids.

ANDY   Yes.

FRIEND   Yeah. I had to almost push my way
                through them.

ANDY   They don't know you.

FRIEND   Then they should show a little more
                respect. One of the little fuckers spat at
                me.

ANDY   Mate.

FRIEND   Really, mate, really spat. Through his
                teeth. Near enough to know it wasn't an
                accident. I turned back at them and they
                were just laughing. I could feel my fucking
                blood rise. What the fuck are you meant to
                do in that situation?

ANDY   Did you provoke it?

FRIEND   There are loads of them. Look out of your
                window. You should call the police, mate,
                seriously. These are the kind of little cretins
                I was protesting against this afternoon.

ANDY	This is my community.
FRIEND	You've forgotten what it feels like. Go out there and you'll feel it. It's the warm evening, mate, it's like a charge.
ANDY	That's not what I see.
FRIEND	Go out there.
ANDY	It's just your perception.
FRIEND	They're not playing, mate.
ANDY	They're just hanging out.
FRIEND	They're kicking stuff around.
ANDY	Are you frightened?
FRIEND	Is that your car, the Skoda?
ANDY	It's fine.
FRIEND	They're too close to your car, mate.
ANDY	There are cars all round the square.
FRIEND	I'm going to move your car, mate.
ANDY	Don't go out again.
FRIEND	You go out, then, you move it.
ANDY	You're in your socks.
FRIEND	Where are you keys?
ANDY	Nothing needs to happen.

A space. ANDY turns the page.

***

ANDY   I want to start a revolution here.

                I met this woman in a bookshop once. I
                was reading a book about The Living
                Theatre. She told me she had been at one
                of their performances in the sixties. She
                told me how, at the end of the performance,
                the audience were led out onto the street
                and encouraged to shout 'Paradise Now!
                Paradise Now!

                Paradise Now! Paradise Now! Paradise
                Now!'

***

FRIEND   You have a 'Child on Board' sign in your
                car.

ANDY   Yes.

FRIEND   What's that about, exactly?

ANDY .   What do you mean?

FRIEND   I mean, are we meant to take notice of it?
As we drive behind you, are we meant to
take notice? Are we meant to think, 'Oh,
must drive more carefully because there's
a CHILD in that car?' Are we meant to
think, 'Oh, a CHILD deserves my fuller
attention because a CHILD is a more
important member of society?' Shit, if
anything, mate, it's the 'child' who survives
the pile up – they're flung clear of the cars
– their little bodies all soft and relaxed and
wobbly, they bounce along the tarmac. Or
am I meant... *(continues)*

ANDY turns the page as the FRIEND continues.

...to think, 'What a smug bastard in the car in front, who the fuck does he think he is trumpeting his parenthood to the world, rubbing the salt into my childlessness.' What the fuck, Andy? It's the most passive aggressive piece of shit.

ANDY   The scholar Jill Dolan has written that the theatre is capable of what she calls utopian performatives.

FRIEND   Fuck sake.

ANDY   She describes these as 'small but profound moments in which the performance calls the attention of the audience in a way that lifts everyone slightly above the present'.

FRIEND   You have a Neighbourhood Watch sticker in your window.

ANDY   It was there when we bought the house.

**

ANDY looks at the friend.

Could we just take a break, mate?

FRIEND	What?
ANDY	A time out, you know? Just a minute. Away from the battle. I'm getting quite bored of it.
FRIEND	Yeah?
ANDY	Yes.
FRIEND	Do you want me to get you some more water?
ANDY	Yes.
FRIEND	From the kitchen?
ANDY	Yes.

The FRIEND exits.

ANDY turns the page.

ANDY looks out at the audience.

I'm doing my best here. I don't really understand what you want though, you know? What do you want?

You're very welcome here, very welcome. It's great to see you. I've cooked some food. I'd love to share it with you. I'd love to sit with you.

The FRIEND returns with a bottle of water and gives it to ANDY. He sits down.

ANDY   I don't appreciate your criticism. I don't think it's helpful.

ANDY has a drink of water.

They sit together for a moment.

OK, thanks.

ANDY turns the page.

***

ANDY   It's 10.30 now.

The sky is becoming a rich purple. And in this small house on a square, facing west, a man waits for his friend, his friend who takes a bottle out of his jacket pocket.

The FRIEND takes a bottle out of his jacket and offers it to ANDY. ANDY takes it and looks at it.

ANDY   Mate. What is that?

FRIEND   A peace offering.

ANDY   That's lovely mate. Where did you get it?

FRIEND   Where d'you think?

ANDY   Did you pay for it?

FRIEND   There's dust on it.

ANDY   Fuck's sake.

ANDY gives the bottle back.

FRIEND   There was no one there.

ANDY   -

FRIEND	Oh, come on, mate. There was no one there. I even called out. That was the first thing on the shelf by the counter. I could have taken anything. I could have scooped up the fags, bottles of gin. I could probably even have opened the till. Fuck's sake. There was no one there, mate. I think I was quite restrained in the circumstances.
ANDY	Grow up, mate.
FRIEND	You used to do the same thing.
ANDY	Not any more.
FRIEND	Cos you can afford not to.
ANDY	Is that what you think?
FRIEND	It's true, isn't it?
ANDY	Did you pay for the wine?
FRIEND	Yes! I paid for the fucking wine.
ANDY	Why didn't you nick the wine too?
FRIEND	I'm not a thief.
ANDY	No?
FRIEND	It was a thrill.
ANDY	And not the wine?

A small space. ANDY turns the page

FRIEND	She came back in.
ANDY	And if she hadn't come back?
FRIEND	Look, I don't fucking know. I didn't know where they were. I called. I don't know them. I don't live here.
ANDY	It's not good, mate. Not cool.
FRIEND	You can't just leave a shop open and go – fuck off down the back and leave it open. Wide open. That's entrapment. You could argue that it's their fault.
ANDY	Take it back, mate.
FRIEND	Fuck off.
ANDY	Seriously. Take it back.
FRIEND	You take it back if you want.
ANDY	Oh, mate.
FRIEND	What the fuck are you? It's nothing. They wouldn't have sold it anyway, it's shit anyway.
ANDY	It's my local shop.
FRIEND	It's Costcutter. It's a chain.
ANDY	Actually, It's a franchise.
FRIEND	Fuck's sake. They don't know you know me. They didn't know who I am.

ANDY   Take it back, mate, it's stealing. You stole something and then you brought it here and you invited me to share in it.

FRIEND   Well, you fucking help me. Get up and help me. I don't know what the fuck I'm doing, do I? I am lost here. Lost. You show me. Come on. Demonstrate - move my arms and legs for me. Come on. I can't move an inch because no direction I look in offers me any kind of fucking answer to how I am. You do it. You fucking do it.

ANDY turns the page, and goes straight into the next speech.

ANDY   There is a theory found in Mayan culture
                        that we are all at the beginning of a new
                        age, an age of separation. A theory that
                        the world really did end in 2012 but that we
                        never actually noticed it.

The FRIEND lies on the floor.

ANDY   A theory that says that we have entered a
                        new phase of history where we slowly drift
                        apart from each other and become isolated
                        and disconnected.

                        But I can't help thinking... I can't help
                        thinking that we're still together here, aren't
                        we?

                                    ***

MUSIC: Penny and the Quarters – You and Me.
ANDY puts his shoes on.
ANDY picks up the bottle and exits.

The FRIEND gets up and sits down on the sofa.

ANDY returns and sits down on the sofa next to him.

They sit together.

The music ends.

FRIEND   Nice table.

ANDY   Yes.

FRIEND   Beautiful table.

ANDY   Thanks. It's from Oslo.

FRIEND   Scandinavian design.

ANDY   Yes.

FRIEND   Nice.

ANDY   Thanks.

FRIEND   And this sofa.

ANDY   Thanks.

A space.

ANDY gets up and goes back to his chair.

ANDY turns the page.

***

The FRIEND throws one of his shoes against the wall.

FRIEND	Fuck, what was that?
ANDY	I don't know.
FRIEND	That was something against your wall.
ANDY	Yes.
FRIEND	That was a stone, mate, or something.
ANDY	Maybe it was a football.
FRIEND	Is your front door locked?
ANDY	I am waiting for my friend.
FRIEND	Do something.
ANDY	I wonder if I am alone.
FRIEND	Call the fucking police.
ANDY	Really alone.
FRIEND	They're outside your house.
ANDY	If really we're all just on our own.
FRIEND	I'm going to have a look.
ANDY	Mate.
FRIEND	They're fucking throwing things.
ANDY	It's a public space.

FRIEND	We're under attack.
ANDY	Just leave it.
FRIEND	I need a cricket bat or something.
ANDY	Just draw the curtains.
FRIEND	A baseball bat.
ANDY	JUST DRAW THE FUCKING CURTAINS AND STAND AWAY FROM THE FUCKING WINDOW.

A space.

ANDY turns the page.

***

ANDY	I am waiting for my friend.
	If you don't mind, we'll wait for my friend.
	He's late. I'd like to apologise on his behalf.

***

	You want to eat something?
FRIEND	Not bothered, mate.
ANDY	I've missed you.
FRIEND	Have you?
ANDY	Yes. I've been looking forward to this.

FRIEND	Yeah?
ANDY	Of course.
FRIEND	I never hear from you.
ANDY	I've been busy.
FRIEND	Thinking?
ANDY	Thinking.
FRIEND	Yeah?

***

The FRIEND clears the stage – removing all the props and furniture.

The FRIEND puts on his shoes.

***

FRIEND   Can I stay here?

ANDY   Where?

FRIEND   Here?

ANDY   In the kitchen?

FRIEND   Fuck off!

ANDY   Where then?

FRIEND   You know.

ANDY   No. Seriously, mate? Where do you mean? Where exactly do you mean?

FRIEND   With you.

ANDY   How long?

FRIEND   Until I get myself sorted.

ANDY   It's not a good time for me.

***

ANDY turns the page.

***

The sky is black now. The limestone walls are cold. The fox has moved on. The houses around the square are quiet. The young people are still on the green, laughing and talking. Their energy hangs in the night.

I look at my friend.

Can I take a cigarette off you?

ANDY exits.

***

The FRIEND moves to ANDY's space. He sits on ANDY's chair. He reads from the script.

FRIEND   We arrive here from some other place, but this is also a place. We listen and watch and we make. We do all of these things together. And then at the end we get up and we leave and we do something. We move somewhere else. To someone or something else. We start again.

My friend is here.

Paradise now. Paradise now. Paradise now.

END